This edition published in 2012 by Maverick House Publishers

Office 19, Dunboyne Business Park, Dunboyne, Co. Meath, Ireland.

http://www.maverickhouse.com
info@maverickhouse.com

ISBN: 978-1-908518-10-1

Text copyright © 2012 Dan Harvey
Internal layout © 2012 Maverick House

'The first way to lose your State is to neglect the art of war'

– *Machiavelli*

To my mother Eva (90), part of that generation which inspires, and in so doing continually challenges us to ask: how did they do it?

About the Author

DAN HARVEY IS A SERVING OFFICER IN THE IRISH Defence Forces. His 30 years of service to date have involved him in a variety of operations both at home and overseas. A highly experienced and respected press officer, he has also pioneered many Defence Forces historical and heritage projects, most notably a number of museum collections. Dan is a constant contributor to *An Cosantóir*, the Defence Forces magazine, and has a keen interest in rugby. He is a former senior player at representative level and now also coaches. He is currently stationed in the Irish Defence Forces Headquarters in Dublin. His first book *Peace Enforcers* was widely received during its publication in 2010. *A Company Action* is his second book.

Table of Contents

Foreword by Kevin Myers

ENOUGH TIME HAS SURELY PASSED FOR US TO BE HONEST about the Niemba ambush, the great baptism of fire of our forces in a foreign field. This was the first time that a stone-age people with stone-age weapons were able to defeat soldiers from the 20th Century. They of course knew the land, and the Irish boys on this strange terrain did not. Moreover, the Irish probably lacked the critical field-craft and fire-support disciplines that might have compensated for these basic disadvantages. This was, classically, an age-old story: a new army, in a new arena, meeting new experiences, the hard way.

The army learnt quickly in response. Carl Gustav submachine guns – far more useful than the old Lee Enfields – were swiftly purchased, and no patrol departed without them. The heavy 'bulls wool' battledress was swiftly improved, if not by straightforward supply from the commissariat then by acquisition from neighbouring UN forces, lawfully or otherwise. One way or another, there would be no more Niembas.

But there remained another issue. Not quite revenge, but reparation; there was the single matter of honour, which all soldiers understand. Armies, at bottom, are organisations in which the maintenance of male pride is paramount. Moreover, there is no pride without honour, and Irish military honour, maintained on a thousand foreign battlefields under many flags that were not Irish, now demanded that Irish military honour be served.

So yes, the subsequent assault by the Irish Army units on a mercenary-led gendarmerie, holed up in a strongpoint called 'the tunnel' in the Congo, which is so brilliantly described in these pages, was done under UN auspices, under a UN flag, and with UN legal authorisation. But I have never heard of a single soldier who went into combat that day against the formidable and well-trained enemy, who hollered, as he advanced into interlocking arcs of enemy fire: UN *go bragh*! Indeed, it's probably fairer to say that those Irish soldiers were driven by one really fine ambition: to restore the military honour of Ireland and the good name of its Army, both in their own minds, and those of their UN masters.

That they succeeded so brilliantly is the reason for this book. Soldiers cannot be peacekeepers unless they are soldiers first, and therefore fighters. Ireland's proud history in UN peacekeeping rests not on the calamity of Niemba but the courage of the men of the tunnel. The self-belief of the army depends upon its ability to kill the enemy. That was what the Battle of the Tunnel was all about, and that is why Dan Harvey's thrilling and scholarly study will remain particularly pertinent.

— Kevin Myers

Acknowledgements

THE GENESIS OF AN IDEA FOR A BOOK CAN BE SUDDEN, inspired by a single dramatic thought, moment or event. Alternatively, it's coming into being can be a gradual and entirely disjointed series of notions unconnected in time, circumstance or place. It can be a collection of individual moments of separate realisations, each a seedling in itself, registering to different degrees before their eventual sum manifest into the makings of a manuscript. So it was that the idea for this text was over two decades in gestation before these considerations collided and connected. In contrast, its first draft once begun was swiftly completed. Framing all this was an innocuous incident some twenty or so years previously on one particular early spring morning after a dreadfully drawn out Irish winter, seemingly forever dreary, dark and damp. With rain and cold still persisting it would nonetheless have been passably mundane but for the added disincentive of my being orderly officer whose role was to initiate, supervise and take responsibility for the security of the barracks. This security was provided for by a mixture of means and measures all overseen by armed personnel. It was these which I considered the lynchpin and I was always mindful to pay my closest attention to them. It was their fitness for duty that underpinned the quality of the day's and night's security. My close inspection then of the on-coming 'for duty' personnel revealed them all to be present, properly equipped and primed, all alert except for one, and he was not in good shape at all. He was the oldest, a sergeant, a veteran of the early 60's, who had seen service in the Congo and was obviously suffering the ill effects of a very heavy night's drinking. I looked at him and he knew I knew. His already bad morning had just got worse. He fully expected to receive a sharp public rebuke; instead I felt of all of us he had probably made the biggest effort to be there. I decided to give his rank and service the benefit of the doubt but didn't let him off the hook completely. I mentioned quietly I'd have a private word with him later. I discreetly called the sergeant aside and firmly suggested he put his second-in-command in charge for a few hours to put himself right, and to never, but never show up for duty like he had again, then promptly got on with my working day.

There's a theory that states work expands to fill the time available, but once you are orderly officer there is never enough time and all through the working day I was hard put to keep up with both the demands of the duty and of my everyday role. Returning to the duty room at the end of the working day I was surprised then when the sergeant approached me apologising for his earlier, now well forgotten by me, un-soldier-like appearance. He earnestly continued that he appreciated how he had been dealt with and in return wished to offer me some sound career advice ... 'Sonnie,' he said, 'STAY OUT OF AFRICA.'

Then some thirty years since the Irish had been

in Congo, the presentations and photos from there mingled in the Officers Mess amongst memorabilia and mementos from other subsequent overseas missions. One such, a Congo painting, hung in a hallway depicting 'The Tunnel', Elisabethville, Congo, December 1961; an altogether uninspiring, unimaginative and unanimated illustration. Nonetheless, its stark austerity provoked if not a fascination, certainly a curiosity. A plaque on its frame listed the names of its contributors, men whom I later interviewed, along with many others during the course of researching this book. One such being the officer father of a cadet class colleague who had related episodes of his own experiences at The Tunnel, so from the very beginning of my military career I had been hearing of the happenings there. A long time ruminating, like a slow burning fuse, it was all to suddenly and dramatically ignite at the Defence Forces 50th Anniversary Commemorations of the Departure to the Congo, in Baldonnel, July 2010, while witnessing the explosive excitement of old comrades meeting – some after many years. Hugs handshakes, hearty laughs, tears flowing freely down cheeks; the honest open happiness of a camaraderie uniquely shared by 'old soldiers'. I resolved there and then to write this story which epitomised the spirit of those early overseas peacekeeping pioneers, to illustrate, as Aristotle put it, that 'character is that which reveals moral purpose exposing the class of things a man chooses to do or avoid'. For if even character was required and evident, it was in facing the dangers of 'real war' on a very wet and dark Congo morning in Elisabethville on 16 December

1961. This book is that story and for its telling I wish to gratefully acknowledge:

Commandant Victor Laing and Captain Stephen Mac Eoin and the ever helpful staff at the Defence Forces Military Archives Section. Commandant David O'Neill and Private Tom McSweeney of the Defence Forces Printing Press. Lieutenant-General (retd) Bill Callaghan, Major-General (retd) Vincent Savino, Major-General (retd) Michael Minehane, Colonel (retd) Tommy Dunne, Colonel (retd) Harry Crowley, Colonel (retd) Sean Norton, Colonel (retd) Peter Feely, Colonel (retd) Michael Shannon, Commandant (retd) George Kirwin, Commandant (retd) Pat Brennan, CQMS (retd) Jim Clarke, Sergeant (retd) Michael Butler, Sergeant (retd) Peter Fields, Corporal (retd) Gerald Francis R.I.P., Private (retd) Pat Lally, Private (retd) John Woolley and Private (retd) John Grace.

I also wish to thank John Mooney, Jean Harrington, Karen Hayes and Claire Wallnutt of Maverick House whose faith in the project was both immediate and consistent throughout. To Maeve O'Connell whose help was invaluable. Finally, to my family for my unavoidable absences that such a project necessitates but nonetheless impacts on valuable spare time available together, that time itself does not replace. I hope I have done all concerned justice.

MAP OF THE CONGO

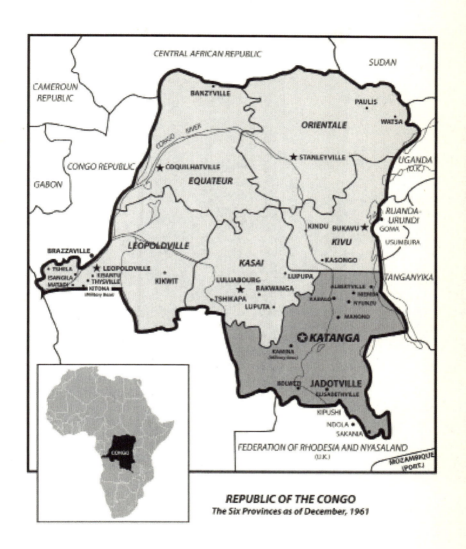

REPUBLIC OF THE CONGO
The Six Provinces as of December, 1961

Katanga Province

ELISABETHVILLE

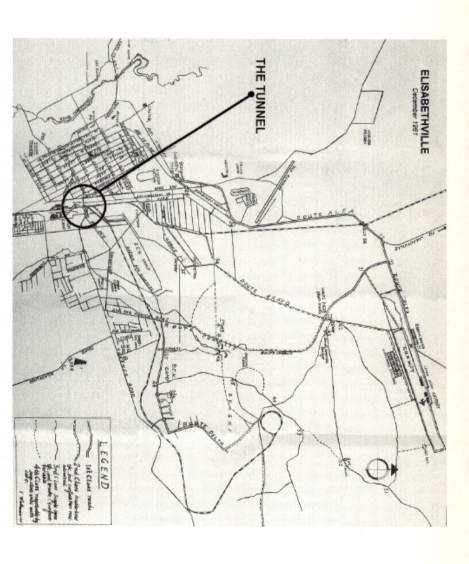

THE TUNNEL

ELISABETHVILLE
December 1961

PLAN OF ATTACK ON THE TUNNEL

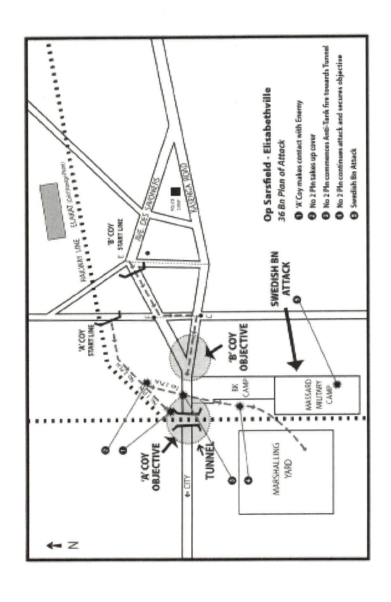

Prologue

8 December 1961

"CRUMP, CRUMP, CRUMP" ... THE INCOMING MORTAR rounds slammed into the Irish camp. It took twenty-six seconds for their firing, flight and fall before they smashed into the Irish position, impacting heavily. The ground shook with their blast effect, the shrapnel scattering, the hot molten metal menacingly seeking its prey, indiscriminately spreading out in search of victims. 'A' Company 36th Battalion, newly arrived, was caught on the wrong side of a mortar barrage. It was savage, raw and violent; deliberate, dangerous and deadly. Corporal Michael Fallon was arbitrarily killed outright. Through sheer chance and circumstance, an unlikely, rare direct hit impacted on the roof of the outhouse building in which he was located. He died almost immediately. The mortar barrage accounted for five injuries also: Sergeant Paddy Mulcahy, Privates Marsh and Gilrain, Troopers Kelly and McMullan. So serious were Trooper McMullan's injuries he had to be medically repatriated home to Ireland because of his wounds. Not yet twenty-four hours proper in Elisabethville, barely two days in the Congo itself, 'A' Company 36th Battalion had suffered one fatality and five wounded. Their arrival the previous day, less lethal, had been only slightly less traumatic.

1

Not Just War But Suicide

7 December 1961

OVER FORTY HITS, TWO OUTBOARD FUEL TANKS punctured, the oil system of the starboard inner Pratt & Whitney engine damaged, the United States Air Force (USAF) Douglas C-124 Globemaster II transport aircraft was one of three which received ground fire on approach to landing at Luena Airport, Elisabethville. This was the beginning of the three-week airlift rotation of the main body of the 36th Irish Infantry Battalion to the Congo to replace the 35th Irish Infantry Battalion – the handover duration being extended due to circumstances arising. The 36th Battalion was the sixth Irish unit to deploy in what had already been a year and a half commitment to what altogether became a four-year involvement, comprising twelve Irish units in all. This rotation was to see the scheduled departure and arrival of some twenty Globemaster aircraft, commencing on the 5 December, ending on Christmas Eve, 1961. Originally destined for Albertville in the Congo's northeast, the twenty-three hour journey took an air route whose flight path went from Dublin over England, France, Italy, the Mediterranean and a first stop at the US Wheelus Field Airbase in Tripoli, Libya for refuelling, then onto RAF-run Kano Airbase in Nigeria, finally arriving at Leopoldville in the Congo. After a day's rest and a further 1200 miles to the south – Congo is a vast country – they reached their destination.

While preparations were underway for landing near Elisabethville, suddenly two UN Indian Canberra jets screamed by discharging their cannons to engage the Katangese Gendarmerie ground positions in the area around the airport. The Globemaster pilots had therefore to carry out landing procedures according to international code, this being when the pilot has not received finalised landing instructions from air-traffic control at the airport control tower. The planes turned into the final leg of their approach and so also out over the hostile Katangese, who let loose a hail of fire from their ground positions. Not yet on the ground, hostilities had begun and 'A' Company were already in the thick of it.

Landing with a trail of aviation fuel vapour behind it spewing from the ruptured fuel tanks, the stricken aircraft made a remarkable landing. More than spectacular, it was miraculous it had not caught fire whilst airborne, considering the heat of the engines and the inflammability of the high octane vapour. There to meet them were those whose own tour of duty had been eventful but was now nearing its end: the men of the 35th Battalion. They were on the apron's tarmac, in the airport's buildings, but mostly in slit-trenches, crawl trenches, weapon-pits and command posts, defending its perimeter. The aircraft's American crews taking in this sight and already shaken by their exposure to incoming fires on final approach commented on the experience that landing in Elisabethville 'wasn't just war, it was suicide'. Of immediate concern also to the aircraft's loadmaster was the real possibility of the soles of the Irish soldiers' hobnail boots causing sparks to fly on contact with the tarmac as they ran from the rear of the plane and igniting the fuel now gushing from the wings and vaporising in the heat. They were extremely fortunate too not to have been engulfed in a flying fireball, as on landing the requirement to apply the breaks often causes sparks, on this occasion none arose and so there were instead no casualties amongst the aircraft's 46 Irish occupants. The planes took off again during the day, the first one on its surviving three engines. The American crew were disinclined to linger in the Congo. For the one hundred and twenty or so newly arrived members of the 36th Battalion, their first impressions could only be stark, yet were only a small taste of things to come.

2

'Sit Rep' (Situation Report)
– Freedom of Movement

'A' COMPANY COUNTED THE PRECISE NUMBER OF bullet holes in the USAF Globemaster's airframe, 48 in all. Still disbelieving of their eventful arrival and bonded in the moment of the shared experience of their good fortune, they quickly ascertained the US aircrew's collective disinclination to remain on the airport's apron to effect repairs. Departure out of Africa if at all possible seemed a far more wise, welcome and attractive avenue to any other alternatives suggested. Giving them a number of boxes of Irish pack rations, they bade them good luck and farewell, then steeled themselves for the new reality they were now faced with. They had hit the ground running and were uncertain where it was leading them. What was certain was the main route leading them out of the airport was considered insecure as sniping continued around the city. Movement to and from the airport for the UN was effected through 'Route Charlie' (Avenue de Aracarios), a less dangerous alternative.

First reports of new developments in Congo came on the 3 and 4 December 1961, two days before departure from Ireland, as Katangese gendarmerie, led by mercenaries, became very active in Elisabethville and on roads leading into the city. All UN and Irish troops were confined to their respective camps. At this stage the intention had been for the 36th Battalion to concentrate in Albertville and the Nyunzu and Niemba areas, but it became necessary to consider a change in plans and to have the 36th take over from the 35th in Elisabethville due to the deteriorating circumstances. The following day the Katangese Gendarmerie placed a roadblock on one of the city's main boulevards, blocking access to the airport. Hardly a random act, in fact its significance was the throwing down of the gauntlet to the UN saying we are going to curtail if not control your freedom of movement. This roadblock was to be removed later after negotiation. However, it was not removed and in addition firing commenced in the city. Irish troops in their camp known as 'Leopold Farm' had to withdraw into closer proximity to the camp due to having been fired upon. A firm decision was taken in light of these new and grave circumstances to redirect the 36th Battalion to effect a relief in place in situ in Elisabethville. The Katangese Gendarmerie together with their white mercenary leaders were determined to ratchet up the pressure on the UN forces. If 'A' Company, newly arrived from Ireland, were in any doubt about the gravity of the situation they were in after the drama of their arrival, it was to become all too obvious over the coming days.

3

A New Departure

IN JULY 1960 THE NEWLY DECLARED REPUBLIC OF Congo became engulfed in violence. The rule of its former Belgian colonists had ceased the previous month and the fleetingly peaceful transition to the country's new Prime Minister – Patrice Lumumba – had imploded. Simmering tribal tensions and internal divisions saw conflict breaking out almost immediately and the difficulties were compounded because the army had mutinied. A lack of key people in the fledgling state's institutions was critical in the dramatic decline. Significantly, mineral-rich Katanga in the south-east, the wealthiest by far of the six Congolese provinces, declared itself independent under Moise Tshombe. The country was economically unviable without it. The Congo, one of Africa's largest countries, 900,000 square miles, nearly the size of Western Europe, with a population of 14 million people was in grave danger of being ripped apart.

The Irish government quickly acceded to a UN request to send a lightly armed infantry battalion to the newly established Opérations des Nations Unies au Congo (ONUC). The aim of the UN troop deployment, which it had been hoped would be short-lived, was to persuade the breakaway province of Katanga and its leader, Moise Tshombe, to re-integrate into the Congo. As the first Irish unit, the 32nd Infantry Battalion was being flown out, the UN was asking the Irish Government for a second such battalion. Ireland's positive response in providing troops to the peacekeeping mission was a new departure and was a courageous decision for the government of the day. This UN involvement was highly noteworthy because it demonstrated that Ireland though small and still young as a State was willing to play its part on the world stage. This was an adventurous undertaking whose scale is impossible to comprehend now. This is a very strange notion, hard for us to grasp some fifty years later, yet half a century ago the almost exotic nature of this international involvement was very tangible and very real.

This new departure was a whole other chapter for the Irish State granting a fresh new perspective on itself and its relationship with the world; it bestowing a newfound sense of self-esteem, pride and identity on independent Ireland. Inwardly also the advent of our UN peacekeeping duty involvement in the Congo helped to heal divisions at home; the lingering divides of the civil war and those of social, religious and economic difference. For the public, Irish soldiers on a foreign field was not a new notion, it had been happening for centuries; this time, crucially, it was as members of its own army, under a UN flag, and the prize was peace. They would learn that they would have to fight or die to win that prize.

4

Chaos in the Congo

CONGO'S MINERAL WEALTH – ITS VAST NATURAL resources – was in stark contrast to its people's poverty. An enormous country, Congo's former colonial history had been brutal. Its recent independence however had swiftly brought it towards, then beyond, the brink of bloodshed. A huge humanitarian tragedy was in the offering and the country itself faced fragmentation. Now Katanga, its primary province, was perched perilously on the precipice of palpable pandemonium.

Seventeen countries' soldiers, including Ireland's – all member states of the United Nations – had contributed to a peacekeeping force attempting to stabilise the situation before it imploded.

That such an undertaking had come to pass owed its origins some seventy-six years beforehand to when the European powers – Germany, Britain, France, Belgium and Italy – at the Berlin Conference hosted by Otto Von Bismark in November 1884 entrusted the Congo, not to Belgium per se, but rather uniquely to the personal control of King Leopold II of Belgium. Unwilling to risk hostilities over the as yet unclaimed regions of Africa, the European colonists were satisfied to amicably divide what was left.

Initially a loss maker, it was shortly to be Congo's bountiful wild rubber that was exploited, resulting in huge personal financial gains for Leopold II by satisfying the demand for tyres for the newly emergent thriving car industry. In their quest for ever increasing quotas of rubber produce, zealous overseers inflicted appalling abuses and atrocities as punishments on the native Congolese when failing to meet these laid down quota amounts.

Congo's abundance of raw materials – timber, ivory, rubber and vast quantities of minerals – were quickly monopolised by Belgian firms paying high dividends to Leopold for the privilege. Inevitably envious competing interest from others, including British businesses unable to gain a highly lucrative market share, exploited the concerns of those outspoken missionaries over the shockingly inhumane treatment of the Congolese and had such concerns raised at the British Parliament whereupon Roger Casement at the British Consul in the Congo was directed to conduct an investigation in mid-1903. By years end, after a thorough, systematic and highly conscientious undertaking, his subsequent report laid bare the maltreatment meted out in graphic detail highlighting the extreme punishments, including the severing of hands which were then preserved by a smoking process, which was proof of money not wasted on bullets. Casement's Report earned him a knighthood, and caused widespread condemnation and criticism of Leopold II. The resultant international hue and cry led to Belgium, the country, been given control of King Leopold II's personal African fiefdom. The horrors did not fade overnight, however.

Diamonds, uranium and other minerals from Congo's seemingly inexhaustible supply soon replaced timber, ivory and wild rubber as income earning exports for the Belgians. It was shortly after World War I that the province of Katanga, where vast resources of copper had been discovered in 1913, attracted fortune seeking European and American mining and mineral firms led by Union Minière, a large Anglo-Belgian concern. Huge sums were fashioned and it became one of the most highly lucrative mining centres globally. It accounted for 50% of Congo's wealth alone. The preservation of its potential ongoing returns focused the attentions of these corporations as the region prepared to enter the countdown to its post-colonial era. Different Colonial countries prepared their respective indigenous populations to ease the transition towards independence; Belgium undertook no such preparations for the Congo. Theirs was the presumption of continuance through utter necessity. Disastrously they believed that the existing white administrative level would continue to administer. There were few Africans in positions of responsibility in the Congo. Its 25,000 man army, Force Publique, was commanded by in excess of one thousand Belgian officers. This, on being granted independence, became the Armée Nationale Congolaise (ANC). Its layer of white command was removed and with it, it has to be said, control. As well as that some two hundred Congolese tribes were just given release from Belgian control.

Granted sudden independence, Congo – with huge mineral wealth but no public administration layer – were unable to impose control on its so-called army to in turn impose stability and security; its new Government's first duty. Chaos resulted. This disintegration arose directly from two speeches, the first by King Bedouin, Belgium's King, the second by Patrice Lumumba, the new Prime Minister of the Congo. In his address to the Congolese, King Bedouin encouraged them to be deserving of the advantages granted on them by his grandfather, King Leopold II, a personage hugely disliked throughout Congo. Insulted, Patrice Lumumba set aside his prepared conciliatory speech, instead delivering an impassioned denunciation of the Belgians in an ardent resounding riposte, which had immediate repercussions. Political opportunists seized the moment, the army mutinied and many tribesmen sought reprisals for generations of white supremacy. There were some ten thousand Belgians living in Congo and many white families, previously associated with mining and plantations, became targeted for robbery, rape and murder. The country's new Prime Minister Lumumba, not anxious to seek the assistance of Belgium, hinted he might contact China. He did in fact communicate with the Russians but, advised by Congo's US Ambassador, instead turned to the UN. The old colonial power, the Belgians, who now had a pretext for intervention – the protection of its citizens – sent in its paratroopers who took possession of Elisabethville, the epicentre of the mineral-rich province of Katanga, one with much international interest. The following day, 9 July 1960, Moise Tshombe declared its independence. Alarmed by possible Russian involvement, the US, at the height of the cold war, put pressure on the UN leadership. Security Council Resolution S/4387 was adopted on 14 July 1960 and within a fortnight the Irish were on their way; marching into the madness of tribal strife, anarchy, and a web of economically-motivated vested self-interests – and it even had an undertow of cold war machinations about it.

Precious metals were at the heart of the madness, some of which were used in the manufacture of jet engines and radar apparatus. Moreover, Katanga supplied a tenth of the world's copper and over half of the world's cobalt. There was also uranium and many minerals including large quantities of diamonds. Thus 10% of the Congo's population generated 50% of the nation's income and the Katangese wanted to protect their interests, as did those European entities that had much to lose and much to gain. Enter the boots of the *Casques Bleus* – the Blue Helmets of the UN – onto Central African soil and headlong into the Congolese maelstrom. The UN was in at the deep end from the beginning. The pace of events was moving rapidly ahead.

5

Reality Check

8 November 1960 Niemba

SUDDENLY, STEPPING OUT ONTO THE TRACK FROM THE dense head-high elephant grass, the Baluba tribesmen quickly formed into a war party. They were carrying bows with arrows whose tips had been dipped in the fatal venom of black mamba snakes, as well as spears, hatchets, knives and clubs.

They strode forward six abreast; there were perhaps forty in all, with as many more in the thick undergrowth. Without warning, they started screaming and shouting as they flung themselves wildly at the hapless eleven-man Irish patrol. Firing a hail of arrows, they set upon the Irish, roaring raucously and yelling. The overwhelming number and aggressiveness of their opponents shocked the unsuspecting Irishmen, who having gone forward of their vehicles to inspect a broken bridge had left most of their weapons in them. The rapidly advancing Balubas had got between the Irish and their two vehicles and had cut off recourse to their means of survival – their weapons – which were agonizingly close yet still out of reach. The Irish patrol, with what few weapons they had, fought for their lives; a desperate defence from being bludgeoned and hacked to death. They quickly succumbed to the suddenness and the savagery. Somehow two survived.

The Niemba Ambush was a seminal moment for Ireland and the Defence Forces. It occurred only three months after the first Irish contingent of two battalions (32nd & 33rd) were deployed amid a mood of national exhilaration. The Irish Defence Forces' involvement in UN overseas service was a national tonic as it heralded the dawn of a new outward-looking, more modern Ireland. The deaths now of nine of its soldiers, the biggest single loss of life in one tragic overseas incident, then or since, in the history of the Defence Forces' overseas story was a stark reality check, a steep learning curve for the Defence Forces and a loss of innocence for Ireland. The dead Irish peacekeepers were given a State funeral, and over a quarter of a million people turned out in Dublin to witness the funeral cortège as it made its way through the capital to Glasnevin Cemetery. The Balubas did not know the Irish would not be belligerent, the Irish did not know the Balubas would be, and so there was chaos in the Congo.

The Niemba Ambush had been carried out by Baluba tribesmen who mistakenly considered that because the Irish troops were white, they presented the same threat posed to them by the white mercenaries in the pay of Moshe Tshombe, a tribal rival. They were soon to learn of the impartiality of the Irish whose own painful history rendered them free of any colonial baggage and in due course provided much needed protection for the Baluba and other tribes in refugee camps. The naivety of an Irish nation was ended, lessons were learned by the Defence Forces, but the drama and the death in the Congo was set to continue.

6

The Frightful Ones – *Les Affreux*

IN AFRICA THE REAL DANGER CAME FROM THE VAST inaccessible terrain, the extreme climate and rampant diseases. In overcoming these enemies the opposing soldiers and peacekeepers had first to stay alive to fight before they could engage any human enemy. For UN peacekeepers belligerence was the enemy, its human form ominously manifest in the many mercenaries in the pay of Tshombe. In southwest Congo Central Africa at the close of 1960 Katanga was at war internally with the Balubas and externally with the ANC (Armée National Congolaise), the army of the newly independent Democratic Republic of the Congo, from which Katanga had been trying to break away. Katanga's president Moise Tshombe significantly strengthened the spine of his force by the addition of hundreds of well-armed, highly trained and combat-experienced mercenaries.

Their presence provided Tshombe with an assertiveness and a disinclination towards a negotiated détente with the UN; instead their existence and the nature of it inevitably catapulted the Katangese towards conflict with the UN forces.

White mercenaries (Belgian, French, British, Rhodesian, South African, some Germans, almost unavoidably one or two Irish), all soldiers of fortune and ex-military adventure-seeking veterans, motivated mostly, if not pure and simply, by money. Ruthless, tough, uncompromising; they were recruited across Europe and elsewhere as 'advisors', 'technicians' and 'police officers' for the Katangan Gendarmerie. Their paid participation granted the secessionists an on-ground tactical and an overall strategic capability; a potency thrusting the Katangese headlong into combat with ONUC.

Mention mercenaries and immediately it evokes an almost romantic mystique; machismo imagery springs to mind, where really words like muscle, malevolence, menace and mayhem ought to more realistically be mentioned. A mercenary is an ex-soldier who sells his military skills for money. A soldier is a member of an army and is trained to fight, to kill. Tshombe recruited hundreds of these 'dogs of war' to bark for him; to deliver a decidedly offensive edge to his pallet of forces, thereby strengthening the overall resolve of his black Katangan Gendarmerie.

An *Evening Herald* article of the time tells its own tale, 'an ex-French Army Officer was being held today on a charge of trying to recruit 'technicians' to work in the troubled Congo province of Katanga. He was held under a law that prohibits recruiting foreign armies on French soil. Police said he had interviewed several men in his hotel room after running this advertisement in local papers:

> CENTRAL AFRICA: Good pay, former soldiers and young men recently discharged. Those having experience in central Africa preferred. With or without speciality, drivers, radiomen, mechanics. Passport necessary, URGENT.

Authorities alleged he paid recruits 1,000 francs (£70) as a bonus to sign. Bachelors were paid 1,970 francs a month and married men 2,190 francs.'

An Irish mercenary recruited by interview in a London hotel answering an advertisement for 'SAFARI GUIDES' enlisted for $800 a month, over six times what he could otherwise earn elsewhere. At the early stages the inducement was less, at $300 a month – officers twice that – but still an attractive enticement and sufficient to draw the interest of many ex-military for hire to the troubled Congo. There were no American mercenaries amongst them as it was generally believed; it was a rumour unsubstantiated in fact, as those who enlisted for military service under a foreign flag were in contravention of US law and could have their passport confiscated.

The mercenaries then amongst themselves naturally fell into three distinct groups: Belgian, French and the English-speakers – the Compagnie Internationale – mostly from the UK, South Africa and Rhodesia. The former two groups, but particularly some of the French amongst them, when off-duty, were given to un-soldierly behaviour that gave rise to an unnecessary notoriety. When in the public eye, some sought attention by courting a macho-type image; unshaven, long-haired, needlessly in possession of many weapons and wearing well worn combats, swaggering from bar to bar in a swashbuckling derring-do fashion.

All this gave rise to an exaggerated impression that they were a collection of ill-disciplined, gung-ho hell-raisers; a representation not lost on the media present and the phrase 'Les Affreux' – the Frightful Ones –

became synonymous with the appearance of some of Katanga's French mercenaries.

In overall command of the mercenaries was a Belgian, Colonel Crèvecoeur, and his second in command was Major Matisse. The French group was under Colonel Faulques, formerly a Major in the Foreign Legion, veteran of Dien Bien Phu and fresh from many encounters in Algeria with the FLN. Bob Denard (Gilbert Bourgeaud) – whose story was widely credited for the feature film *The Wild Geese*, and the novel *Dogs of War* by Frederick Forsyth – was involved. The Compagnie Internationale was initially commanded by Englishman Dick Browne, whose brother was a Tory MP with Mick Hoare and Alistair Wicks amongst them. Sometimes confused early on with a unit called the White Legion, this much smaller mercenary outfit were, however, destined to be taken prisoner by UN Ethiopian troops at Kabala in northern Katanga.

Very well equipped, mercenary armament included brand new weaponry from Belgian manufacturers such as the 7.62mm FN rifle (British equivalent SLR, or American M16), the belt-fed 7.62mm General Purpose Machine Gun (GPMG), the FN Browning 9mm High Power Pistol, the 9mm Vigneron M2 and the FN 9mm UZI submachine guns.

Speed, noise and immense firepower were the tactics employed by the mercenaries to counter the Baluba. Noise was associated with great power and conveniently was a by-product of firepower which was used to maximum effect to saturate any Baluba target areas, whether real, possible or even simply suspected. The speed was achieved by being organised into several Units known as 'Groupes Mobiles'. At the forefront of each were up to six 'Willy's Jeeps' heavily armed with a mounted GPMG or a .3 or .5 Browning Heavy Machine Gun (HMG). With its heavy barrel, the .5 was an updated model of the 1930s design. Two million had been manufactured initially and it remains one of the most powerful machine guns in existence. Irish troops were to encounter it, or more precisely, were subjected to its highly disruptive effect and initially had little equivalent viable response. These highly mobile columns were sometimes spearheaded by light armoured vehicles. Whether jeeps or armoured, or a mix, these were supported by truck-borne Katangese gendarmerie. The required speed, firepower (noise) and accuracy were delivered in many whirlwind attacks to good effect.

Communications were provided by the PRC9 short-range backpack radio sets used by the US army and powerful radio transmitters used as rear-links when the various Groupes Mobiles were operating in the Bushveld (a dense bush-filled region in Southern Africa) or hemmed in along routes by impenetrable jungle forests, to communicate with the État Major (Gendarmerie/mercenary headquarters in Elisabethville) at ranges of up to several hundred kilometres.

The mercenaries were employed to 'pacify' the Balubas and take on the Central Government's ANC. In the first instance fighting unsophisticated Balubas demanded an unorthodox approach because of the cultural nature of their comprehension. Uncomplicated, badly organised, poorly armed they could however be fanatically brave. Frequently fortified by marijuana and heavily influenced by tribal witch doctors, their tactic was ambush or frontal assault in overwhelming numbers. The prospect of falling prisoner to the Baluba was inconceivable as they were known to practice grotesque ritual torture with savagery, barbarism and callousness causing the victim excruciating pain and suffering before an unimaginable death. These were dire deeds and happenings in the heart of darkness. Neither had the Irish been immune, their eleven-man patrol having been attacked and nine butchered at or near Niemba, yet within a matter of some eighteen months it was Irish and Swedish UN troops that were to defend Baluba refugee camps in Elisabethville during the fighting of 1961 and 1962. At one point some 40,000 Baluba and other tribal refugees were under their protection.

The Baluba had once formed a mighty empire larger than Belgium and Holland combined which had since waned and were living as a minority tribe in northern Katanga with a rival, now more powerful tribe, the Lunda. The Bayeke too, fierce and warlike, were a third and strong tribe to contend with. Ancient tribal rivalries continued to exist. Tshombe was a member of the Lunda royal house and so a natural rival of the Baluba. Since gaining independence unrestricted by Colonial subjection or obedience to tribal permissions ,the Baluba Jeunesse (young adult Balubas) had rampaged across northern Katanga attacking white Belgian settlers and black tribal rivals armed with rudimentary weapons. Elementary, primitive and crude, these included poisoned arrows and spears, clubs studded with six-inch nails, and sharpened bicycle chains which could shred human flesh to the bone.

Getting to grips internally with the Baluba was one

thing – and ongoing – but the time would surely come for military assertiveness in support of the secession. Set against the backdrop of the powerful and competing influences already tearing the Congo apart – nationalism, tribalism, idealism and commercialism – crucially three critical circumstances – the death of Congolese Prime Minister Patrice Lumumba; a second UN Security Council Resolution; and the increased activity of the ANC – resulted in events unfolding fast.

In December 1960, through duplicity, deception and double-dealing, Patrice Lumumba along with two others (Maurice Mpola and Joseph Okito) were arrested by Colonel Joseph Mabutu and President Kasavubu of the Leopoldville Government and delivered into the hands of his tribal and political opponents resulting in the announcement of their deaths on 13 February by the Katangese Minister of the Interior, Godefroid Munongo. Seven days later, on 21 February 1961, the UN Security Council adopted a new resolution allowing the ONUC to use force to restore order and take whatever steps necessary to prevent civil war erupting in the Congo. The UN resolution also demanded the immediate evacuation of all mercenaries and other foreign military and political advisors. The authority for 'the use of force, if necessary, as a last resort' was a mandate to act, hugely significant, changing the nature of the UN forces' Rules of Engagement from passive peacekeepers (opening fire as a last resort and only if fired upon), to active peace-enforcers allowing a more robust, vigorous, proactive posture. Finally, under Mobuto, the ANC increased their activities, particularly along the internal provincial borders of Kasai and Katanga. Into this turmoil Irish Lieutenant General Séan McKeown was appointed Force Commander to ONUC in January 1961. Order continued to further deteriorate throughout the Congo following the period of Lumumba's death from early to mid 1961. Late in August his replacement, Mr Cyrille Adoula, was elected as the new Prime Minister of the Congo. He immediately announced his intention to end the Katangan secession effort and special legislation was enacted to allow the Congolese government to expel foreign officers and mercenaries. To achieve this Adoula requested the assistance of the UN force sent in to keep the peace and maintain order. In effect he was requesting a more partisan participation than the UN force and its contributing members had anticipated. He wished them to become more measurably immersed in the internal fighting than they intended, to take on a deeper dimension with the developing drama. Had the innocent UN been manipulated towards mission creep unwittingly, allowing an escalation of its role or was it simply that this was what maintenance of order required? For sure, order within Congo could not be restored until the Katangan secession threat was addressed and order within Katanga could not be restored until the menace of the mercenary threat was addressed.

7

'SMASH'
The First Battle of Katanga
– September 1961

IMMEDIATE ACTION IN THE LIKELY EVENT OF COMING into harms way is to first remove the source of danger. Before dawn on 28 August 1961 the UN's Irish, Swedish and Indian battalions were out in force and active in Elisabethville, their objective to pre-emptively oust the foreign military and white mercenaries from the Katangese Gendarmeriés order of battle. The logic of the surprise UN offensive was to outwit them now rather than having to overpower them later. Operation Rampunch, which became known as Operation Rumpunch, was the UN's direct response to the ever increasing belligerent behaviour of the Katangese. The UN was taking the mercenary fuel from the Katangan fire to contain the Congolese flames. All mercenary, foreign military and paramilitary forces were targeted for arrest. It was an attempt to reduce the kinetic effect potential of Tshombe, his Katangan Regime, and his mercenary-led military force. By defusing his military power and prowess it could cause him to seek a negotiated settlement more earnestly. For the previous six months (January to July 1961) peace talks had – frustratingly – not yielded the desired results and Irishman Dr Connor Cruise-O'Brien, appointed UN Special Representative in Katanga by UN Secretary General Dag Hammarskjöld, was charged to deliver a solution to the reintegration of Katanga back within the Congo. Thwarted by Tshombe's evident determination to keep Katanga independent, Cruise-O'Brien was equally – and as stubbornly – determined to bring the secession to an end. Tshombe and his overseas advisors were hoping to outlast the UN initiative knowing the UN for its part was in its early days of pioneering its peacekeeping policies, making them match their on-ground coordination of its military political and diplomatic strategies. The Katangan secession was backed by European commercial patronage whose own interests lay in ensuring that Katanga's wealth did not fall into the hands of Congolese nationalists. A more forceful posture was required to demonstrate that the UN was serious about ending Katanga's succession; Operation Rampunch was launched. Well organised and effective, the UN rounded up many of Elisabethville's off-guard mercenaries with no casualties suffered or inflicted and very few shots fired. The pattern was the same throughout Katanga. Initially it was resounding success; all of the operations' military objectives were achieved, the majority of the mercenaries were captured, Godefroid Munongo, the Interior Minister, had been placed under house arrest and control of a number of installations was wrestled from gendarmerie hands. The UN in staging their show of strength had demonstrated their willingness to forcibly implement the resolution of 21 February and – temporarily at least – seized the initiative from Tshombe. Meanwhile in north Katanga, another Irish unit, the 1st Infantry Group, had taken over command of Kamina base on the 4 August. Their tasks were airfield defence, base defence and its approaches, general administration of the base and protection of Kilubi Dam and its hydroelectric station located some sixty miles north east of Kamina base. In pursuance of that task 'B' Company, 1st Infantry Group, had taken over Kilubi on the 16 August. Lieutenant Michael Minehane (later Major-General and Force Commander in UNIFCYP 1992/94) remembers:

Things took a serious turn from the 19 August onwards when headquarters in Leopoldville organised what was known as Operation Rampunch. This was UN's plan to haul in all the white mercenaries in Katanga, detain them, and repatriate them. For us, that required the immediate setting up of a Detention Centre in Kamina and it also meant that we must be prepared for the hostility which it would give rise to in the Kamina area. The Detention Centre was prepared and our defences were upgraded in anticipation of the inevitable reaction that it would provoke. Detention started in all of Katanga on the 28 August and within days we were hosting [as prisoners] *150 men. Tension mounted in Kamina and in the rest of Katanga. Detaining that many rogues created problems for us and we were happy to see a couple of Sabena 707s airlift them out of Kamina between the 9 and 14 September. By 14* [September] *we had serious concerns about the intentions of the gendarmerie battalion in Kaminaville. Our unit had its first experience of action within days. Nobody in their wildest imaginings could have forecast that an attack would come from the air, but it did! A Fouga jet appeared over the base and indicated to our observation tower that he intended to attack us. The pilot discussed likely targets and his general intentions with the staff of the tower. We had to consider some form of defence against this unexpected threat. The best we could come up with was our Vickers MMGs which were mounted by our two artillery officers in an anti-aircraft mode for which they were never intended and ill suited. Nonetheless, fire was directed at the Fouga on its next visit. In all, the Fouga paid us about six visits during which he strafed airport buildings and defensive positions. On his second visit to us the pilot indicated that he intended to do damage, that the joking was over. Sure enough he selected a DC3 on the runway and offloaded his hardware on it. He scored a bull's-eye and the plane went up in flames. This was pretty serious and we were left to ponder the future without defence against a developing and serious threat. He represented our very first taste of warfare, our first shots fired in anger. It was truly a benign introduction to fighting but for any soldier it was a singular experience.*

Sporadic fighting had broken out in Elizabethville. In the following days there had been heavy exchanges of fire in that city. At Kamina [base] we were aware of rumblings to the south in Kaminaville. Troops were assembling and their area of interest could only be the strategically important airbase at Kamina. They were eventful days and for me they were about to become even more eventful. My area of responsibility within the company was the support weapons i.e. MMGs and our tiny 60mm mortars. The company was commanded by Commandant Kevin Mac Mahon and my platoon was commanded by Captain Thomas Hartigan. On the late evening of the 14 September 1961 I was called to Kevin's office where I received a brief, to the effect that the Swedes at Kaminagate were under attack by the gendarmerie, and were in dire need of support. Since mortars were my business Kevin instructed me to get on up there and give them a hand. Mortars come in a variety of sizes. At 60mm, my three mortars were the smallest made and not likely to impress the Swedes as serious support. We had to help them and soon I was on my way with a crew of Sergeant McCabe, Private Jack McGrath and others.

We rendezvoused with a guide at about ten in the evening and some three miles south of the base. I remember it as a beautiful moonlit night and I vividly recall all the sounds of an African evening, especially the crickets. I remember too as we moved towards the Swedish position the voice of a Swedish radio operator, in our vehicle, calling to his base 'Alpha Rudolf, Alpha Rudolf, kum, kum'. Movement forward to the Swedish position was eerie and worrying, since we were in totally strange territory. However, we were led in safety by our Swedish guide. We were extremely happy to find prepared mortar trenches located in a very suitable place just to the rear of the Swedish forward trenches.

Early in the day a company-sized detachment of gendarmes had tried to penetrate the base along the road. The Swedes fought well and held off the attack. The gendarmerie took casualties and backed away, leaving behind a large truck laden with ordnance. As dawn broke I was able to observe the truck some 300m from our positions. Its driver was dead in the cab and on top of the cab was another dead soldier who had been manning a machine-gun, mounted atop the cab. As the light improved it was possible to see that the gendarmerie were making serious efforts to recover their truck and it's ordnance. By that time my crew was set up and ready for whatever came our way. The Swedish commander came and talked to me about neutralising the truck with mortar fire. I advised him that while he was asking the impossible, we would give it a *go. The mortar is essentially a neutralising weapon. It is not a pin-point target weapon. Even the idea of targeting a truck at the distance seemed fanciful. In true artillery style we bracketed the truck — one round just beyond, then one round short and the next landed smack, bang on the truck. The Swedes were delighted and, needless to say, full of admiration for our skills (good fortune)!*

SEVENTY-THREE MERCENARIES WERE ARRESTED — 41 BY the Irish — in the province throughout the first day of Operation Rampunch and by 8 September, 273 non-Congolese personnel in the Katangan Gendarmerie (mercenaries and Belgian officers) had been repatriated with some 65 awaiting a similar departure. In all, over 75% of known mercenaries in Katanga were arrested and flown out by the UN. 'The game was up' was how matters were generally believed to be amongst the mercenaries, although it was estimated 104 had slipped the net. The military momentum gained as a result of Operation Rampunch was, however, neither politically nor diplomatically maintained, and so lost. Mistakenly, the UN allowed local and Belgian officials to complete the measures the UN had initiated, but these proved unsuccessful. While the operation did see off the larger part of the Belgian Officer Corps of the Katangan Gendarmerie with additional UN pressure on Belgium, those deported mercenaries flown out by the UN were directly, although discretely, flown back in by Tshombe, only in additional numbers — the game was very much back on.

A by-product of the operation — of no small

future significance – was the seizure of 14 assorted Katangese aircraft (two Sikorsky helicopters, three Alouttes helicopters, three Dakotas, four Doves and two Herons). Five aircraft (two Fouga Magister Jets, two Doves and a Tri-pacer) not at Elisabethville escaped impoundment. Still, virtually their entire air compliment had fallen uncontested into UN hands. However seriously diminished, the skies were still the preserve of the mercenary pilots and albeit much reduced, air superiority remained to be enjoyed by them; in the land of the blind, the one-eyed man is king. With no UN fighter aircraft available, the Katangan Fouga Magister was master. This combat jet trainer from Aerospatiale, somewhat obsolete, remained unrivalled in the Congo skies. Swallow-like in appearance with its highly distinctive butterfly tail, its cruising speed was 750 km/h and it had a range of almost 1,000 km. It could strike any target with its rockets and 7.62mm machine guns or bomb it at will; altogether was a lethal force multiplier. A lone Fouga was itself a serious single prospect to have to deal with and in the hands of the stocky Flemish-Belgian mercenary pilot Magain, UN ground forces were particularly vulnerable and susceptible to its armaments.

After Operation Rampunch a vicious campaign of anti-UN propaganda was conducted by the Katangese government. As well as this anti-UN demonstrations were orchestrated in the centre of Elisabethville, there was increased gendarmerie activity and a noticeable intensification in the presence of mercenaries around the city. On the 9 September road blocks sprang up throughout the capital to impede UN movement and the following day in Jadotville (Likasi), a quiet mining town 160 km north of Elisabethville, a very large mercenary-led gendarmerie force of over 2,000 cut off an isolated company of 157 Irish troops in what was to become known as the Siege of Jadotville. The Irish troops 'A' Company of the 35th Battalion (predecessors of the 36th Battalion), hugely outnumbered, bravely held their ground and valiantly fought it out against impossible odds and circumstances for four days (13 to 17 September); only lack of ammunition, water, rations and with no re-supply nor reinforcements in prospect rendered their position untenable. Meanwhile back in Elisabethville, a pending refugee problem fast developing, having already assumed large proportions, was set to grow bigger still. All of these forces working in opposition gave rise to a dramatic escalation in tension and a taut atmosphere, Elisabethville was on edge. Operation Morthor, a Hindu word meaning to smash or a hammer blow, was conceived. It was to be Operation Rampunch with lessons learned but the Katangese and their mercenaries had learned hard lessons too. For the UN, Katangan secession was to be smashed, dealt a decisive hammer blow; for the Katangese, secession was to be maintained by all means possible. Such circumstances begot the first battle of Katanga. The province itself was huge, approximately 500 miles from east to west, and 700 miles from north to south, in all about ten times the size of Ireland. This involvement meant the Irish became experienced in areas and distances almost beyond the understanding of a people born on a small island.

If Operation Rampunch succeeded in its aim of

outwitting the Katangese, Operation Morthor, two weeks later, did not enjoy the same success in its aim of overpowering them. Launched at 2.00am on 13 September, there were six specific targets for three eager UN battalions with one planned outcome. Frustratingly, it did not happen as anticipated, instead there was more conflict encountered and less success achieved. The Katangan Gendarmerie and mercenaries were waiting and had a score to settle. Unlike Rampunch with only a few rounds fired, this time out there were many. Neither was it trouble-free, instead there were difficulties, heavy fighting, injuries and fatalities. It was initially successful, with the Irish battalion's objectives being achieved within two hours without encountering resistance. With their newly occupied positions secured, Radio College and the tunnel, it was becoming more and more obvious with the rising crescendo of fires all about them that militarily all was not progressing smoothly. The Indian battalion had become involved in heavy street fighting at the Post Office and at Radio Katanga. Strong Katangese gendarmerie resistance was met and after eventually capturing the two positions, a number of counter attacks and much sniping had to be withstood. The Indian battalion had received armoured car support from the Irish and Swedish. The Irish Ford armoured car looked the part, but wasn't. It raised concerns. Home-built in Carlow, it was manufactured from plate steel salvaged from old industrial boilers from the Liffey Dockyard, this was not hardened steel and so offered insufficient protection from heavy rounds. It had a Ford V8 petrol engine set in the chassis of a three-tonne Ford truck. It was rear-wheel drive with a high centre of gravity, its circular turret design derived from the British Lancia armoured car of the War of Independence era. Top-heavy, its manoeuvrability suffered. It was armed with the 303 Vickers Machine Gun whose application was far more suited to its original use as a static field support weapon than its adaptation for use in the armoured car; being water-cooled the transition restricted its use to short sharp staccato bursts. Its capability was not to be dismissed completely however, the Ford played a very useful role in patrolling, reconnaissance and fire-support. Unfortunately it was absolutely no match for the American-built Staghound with its 8mm of hardened steel protective armour and its lethal 37mm gun in use with the Katangese. In the upcoming rotation of the 35th and 36th Battalions four Ford armoured cars were left behind in Dublin airport during the subsequent airlift, due to restrictions on space. Most of the UN battalions' early objectives secured, albeit those of the Indian Dogra's (the Indian contingent had both Dogra and Gurkha battalions within it) only after hostilities were overcome, meant the operations' prospect of overall success were heightened. This early optimism caused a premature radio confirmation by Dr Conor Cruise-O'Brien of Congolese Central Government claims that 'the secession of Katanga is now over'. In fact the mercenaries, many freshly recruited, were more numerous than first thought and had opted for 'shoot and scoot' tactics, preferring to go hit and run than head-on with the UN. The fighting was thus set to continue, sporadic in nature, and concurrently more widespread than heretofore. Crucially, the Katangese still enjoyed air superiority and were to employ it to telling effect at Jadotville, Lufira Bridge and Elisabethville. That UN ground forces were without air cover and highly vulnerable to machine gun fires, bombs, and rockets ranging from the skies, was a major consideration when planning, tasking and undertaking tactical moves and manoeuvrings. News was also beginning to filter through of the 'A' Company's precarious predicament in Jadotville: that Tshombe had been missed, having – it was believed – escaped in the back of an ambulance. Also worrying was a lack of radio communications with the Irish at the Radio College. There were growing fears they may have been overwhelmed and captured. They were. The Irish patrol subsequently sent out to investigate was ambushed, while the Irish holding the tunnel were now coming under machine gun and mortar attack. Meanwhile, the plight of 'A' Company at Jadotville was deteriorating rapidly as a full frontal assault situation was developing in earnest. The Indian battalion was now exchanging heavy fire with the gendarmerie and mercenaries at Tshombe's palace. All in all it was becoming increasingly likely that the UN offensive's impetus was culminating. Under pressure, UN commanders struggled to keep abreast of the confusion of the many unfolding combat scenarios, trying to interpret the operational picture, one becoming increasingly challenging as it was changing rapidly and most often not for the better. Instead it threw up new difficulties and dilemmas, in hindsight some of their own making. Lieutenant (later) Colonel Michael Shannon, was platoon commander of Number Six Platoon 'B' Company of the 35th Battalion. Before

'A' Company arrived to Jadotville, he and his platoon had been sent there as advance party for the subsequent arrival of the remainder of his 'B' Company.

Once there, he met nine members of the recently departed Swedish company who themselves left shortly thereafter. It became apparent very quickly the white settlers of Jadotville who they were supposedly sent to protect resented them being there and as soon as the full complement of 'B' Company arrived made this openly plain by mounting a full demonstration protesting the UN presence there. It was abundantly clear there was no mission to be achieved; as the first platoon in, his was the first out, the remainder of 'B' Company following.

It was incomprehensible to him then when on his arrival back in Elisabethville he met his counterpart of 'A' Company preparing to depart en route to Jadotville to perform the mission his company and that of the Swedish before had deemed unnecessary and unachievable, in isolation without mutually supporting force available. The two young Irish lieutenants could only wonder at the muddled confused thinking behind that decision, one which was to have 'B' Company with Swedish armoured car support racing back the 80 miles north to now give assistance to the beleaguered 'A' Company. 'Force Kane One' was on its way only to have to come to an abrupt halt at the Lufira Bridge 20 miles short of their destination, their route blocked by improvised obstacles and tree stumps and, as with all good ambushes, covered by mercenary interlocking fire.

'A' Company were in peril, the hastily assembled

relief force had its orders. The instruction came to push through, 'go for it', the lead armoured vehicle gave support fire, the second got stuck on the bridge, tree stumps got caught up under the wheel arch of first one, then the second vehicle. The attempted break through to Jadotville under Commandant Johnny Kane floundered. Only an heroic reaction under Lieutenant Michael Shannon which saw Corporal John Kavanagh earn a DSM, dismounting and using a plank from the bridge to free the obstructions, all the while under fire, allowing them and their crews to withdraw safely. Thereafter Lieutenant Shannon acted as FOO (Forward Observation Officer) directing mortar fires from Captain Cyril McQuillan's support platoon of Battalion HQ onto likely gendarmerie positions. This and a later attempt 'Force Kane Two' with Indian Ghurkha troops came under attack and was beaten back by both mercenary reinforcements and the Fouga Magister which stopped them in their tracks. The column in retreat was later ambushed. 'A' Company were left to win the firefight and inflicted heavy fatalities on their attackers over four days only to have to negotiate a cease-fire and face captivity (unimaginably with no casualties themselves) having demonstrated immense bravery. Some 33 years later, on his last overseas posting before retirement(an EU posting), now Colonel Michael Shannon, who was involved with election supervision in South Africa in 1994, was one evening at a bar in Johannesburg and met up with what turned out to be a number of ex-mercenary participants in Congo. On discovering he was Irish, in the military, and had been in the Congo and at Lufira, they commented 'your mortars killed upwards of thirty of our guys', little realising they were talking to the FOO who had directed the fires onto them; he little realising just how deadly accurate his instructions had been.

With 'A' Company holding their ground valiantly, 'Force Kane One' still attempting break through, activity was ongoing in Elisabethville but it wasn't going the UN's way. An Irish soldier, Trooper Edward Gaffney, was killed when he drove his Bedford truck into crossfire. The ambushed patrol, en route to the Radio College, had its Ford armoured car disabled by an anti-tank round believed fired under the command of mercenary Bob Denard. It was subsequently restarted by two injured crew, Corporal Nolan and Trooper Pat Mullins. It is believed that they took a wrong turning and were ambushed, with Trooper Mullin's body remaining undiscovered to this day.

Initiative stalled, it became clear the fighting resulting from Operation Morther would not bring about a forced solution on the secession. The UN had to now consider its options: fight on, negotiate or withdraw. It became clear the middle option was the preferred course of action when it became known that Dag Hammarskjöld, the Secretary General of the UN was en route to broker a ceasefire. Mysteriously his plane crashed. He and 15 others on board died. His death shocked the world.

Ireland was deeply involved in the Congo crisis. Lieutenant General Sean McKeown was in command of all UN peacekeeping troops there to support the government in its efforts to prevent Katanga from seceding. Dr Conor Cruise-O'Brien was Hammarskjöld's special representative in Katanga. A battalion of Irish soldiers was engaged in heavy fighting and had suffered fatalities and casualties, some were now held prisoner.

In the wake of these dramatic events a ceasefire was agreed by the UN and Katanga which took effect on 21 September 1961. Economic sanctions were imposed on the UN force by Katangese authorities. Electricity, telephone and water were cut off. Fresh food supplies had to be flown in. Mr Frank Aiken, Ireland's Minister for External Affairs, arrived on 23 September and visited the scenes of the recent fighting. An exchange of UN prisoners was agreed but took some time to put into effect. It was 25 October before the Irish prisoners – 183 all ranks and 3 civilian interpreters – were handed over at the old airstrip on the outskirts of Elisabethville. The tunnel, the post office and the radio station (at Kilobelabe) were evacuated. A negotiated cessation of Katanga's secession was now unlikely and a UN withdrawal unthinkable; consideration was now leaning towards the enforcement of a more military solution. On 24 November in the halls of the UN a number of resolutions were debated and agreed, one of which conferred on the new Secretary General UThant all necessary powers to expel the white mercenary advisors and parliamentary forces from Katanga; a final showdown in Katanga was looming. Men, material and munitions were moving; the UN was gearing up for 'real war'.

8

An Uneasy Peace

THE EVIDENT ABUNDANCE OF BACKBONE DISPLAYED BY
the Irish at Jadotville was in stark contrast to the dearth
of political street wisdom that placed them there. An
unease existed that the predicament may have been
made manifest by Belgian manipulations in the UN
forum, machinations to the effect ONUC needed to
address the security of isolated white settlements in
Katanga. The tactical deployment of an organisation's
military assets ought to serve its political strategic aims
in the first instance and not be able to be unscrupulously
manoeuvred by others to their advantage. Troubling
also was the UN forces' inappropriately resourced
military capabilities to match the assigned tasks; the
mission's overall objectives had often seemed uncertain,
confused and ill-defined, while the dithering of the
decision-making adversely impeded the speed of the
necessary military planning. Even more unsettling were
the unexplained enigmatic circumstances surrounding
the mystery of the tragic Dag Hammarskjöld plane
crash. Accidental, maybe; suspicious, certainly;
speculation, endless. In theatre, of enormous and
immediate concern was that relations between the UN
and Katanga Government had greatly deteriorated by
the beginning of December. Katangan gendarmerie had
established a number of road blocks in the south of the
city of Elisabethville, denying freedom of movement in
that direction to the UN. Subsequent to the series of

unsuccessful negotiations, his stalled imposition of an imposed solution in the guise of operations Rampunch and Morthar, and the death of Dag Hammarskjöld in the plane crash, Dr Conor Cruise-O'Brien sought to voluntarily release himself from his UN assignment in Katanga and departed the Congo. On the 5 December, with 'A' Company busily boarding the three USAF Globemasters at Dublin Airport to commence the 36th Battalion rotation from Ireland, there were reports in the newspapers of an impromptu press conference held in his New York hotel room the previous evening where Dr Conor Cruise-O'Brien accused the British of covert support for President Tshombe with the aim of getting his regime recognised.

Meanwhile, also on the 5 December in Elisabethville itself, the issue of the removal of the roadblocks was spontaneously combusting. Three days previously a road-block was set up in the tunnel by Katangan gendarmerie and a number of UN personnel were 'arrested'. Two Irish officers were fired on near the road-block but escaped uninjured. The following day a Swedish UN car was also fired upon, killing the driver and wounding three others. Twenty-four hours later another road-block was erected at the roundabout on Avenue Saio-Stanley, a particularly sensitive spot lying on the route from UN headquarters to the airport. A strong Swedish patrol failed to have this obstacle removed.

An outright attack was launched on the gendarmerie-held roundabout by a company of Indian Ghurkhas and a mixed unit of one Irish platoon under Lieutenant Tom Quinlan with two Ford armoured cars, two sections of Ghurkhas and one Swedish APC, all under the command of an Indian, Captain Salaria. This latter force was ambushed near the old air-strip while en route about one mile from the roundabout but after a skirmish succeeded in joining up with the Indian Ghurkha company and together reclaimed and freed the Avenue Saio-Stanley roundabout from gendarmerie possession at the overall cost of one UN soldier killed and 28 gendarmerie. The same day (5 December), sniping began into the Irish HQ, Leopold Farm, with sporadic mortar fire in the vicinity. Within 24 hours with 'A' Company 36th Battalion in the air en route to Congo, the bullets were flying in Elisabethville. Also flying overhead, UN jet fighters appeared for the first time. While they did not fire, their presence had a striking effect on the morale of the UN force, particularly the Irish. The bitter memories of the September fighting during Operation Morthor and the handicaps imposed by a single unopposed Fouga Magister Katanga fighter over Jadotville, Lufira and Elisabethville were now assuaged. Now there was an answer to the Katangan strafing and bombing. As a result the few Katangan planes left, confined themselves to night flying, and bombing was happily inaccurate.

The Irish strength in Elisabethville was now very low. Most of 'A' Company (72 all ranks) had been rotated out since 29 November, the 35th Battalion's 'B' Company was in Nyunsu and 'C' Company in Niemba, northern Katanga province, leaving only 'HQ' Company, the armoured car group, and a platoon plus of 'A' Company 35th Battalion. This had been the date appointed for the final rotation of the

35th Battalion. All preliminary packing, documentation and arrangements had been completed, but plans had to be altered as a result of the situation erupting around them. In the event, final rotation did not start until 18 December. At 2.05pm the following day, 7 December, the 36th Battalion began to arrive, greeted by a hail of incoming fire, nearly knocking their lead aircraft from the skies on final approach to landing at Elizabeth airport. Lieutenant Colonel Michael Hogan Officer Commanding 36th Battalion, elements of his battalion staff and two platoons of 'A' Company entered Leopold Farm (the Irish camp) and were greeted with a very noisy fire-fight immediately outside the post. Fire had been directed at the Irish camp since early morning. At 7.30am five mortar bombs dropped in the camp and fire continued during the morning. An Irish UN patrol went out with the objective of locating the source of the firing. This patrol was unsuccessful and the Katangese pushed forward and were engaged by camp defence. They were beaten off just as the 36th Battalion arrived in camp. While having a meal in the mess the roof of Leopold Farmhouse was hit by a 37mm shell and Lieutenant Colonel Hogan's plate was covered in ceiling plaster and debris. Firing by Katangese snipers, machine guns and mortars continued sporadically throughout the afternoon and also through the night. Indian 4.2 inch mortars located at the Swedish camp fired throughout the night; some 300 rounds on the tunnel and Katangese gendarmerie Camp Massard. The Irish were in the direct line of this fire and sleep was out of the question, especially for the newly-arrived, uninitiated members of the 36th Battalion on their first night in Katanga in rain-filled trenches around the camp's perimeter. The harassing of the Irish continued again the next morning with sniping, mortar and machine gun fire. A fighting patrol was again dispatched and this time a number of snipers were cleared from nearby villas and a group of gendarmerie, estimated at company strength, was routed; however, a mortar bomb scored a direct hit on an out-house building in Leopold Farm killing Corporal Michael Fallon and wounding five other members of the 36th Battalion. An uneasy peace shattered, the second Battle of Katanga had begun and unknown to the men of the newly arrived 'A' Company they were all too soon to take centre stage.

Operation UNOKAT
The Second Battle of Katanga
(5 – 21 December 1961)

9

Point 'E' – Liege Cross Roads

THEIR PATIENT DETERMINATION TO KILL PAID OFF; the Katangan Gendarmerie ambush set on Stanley Avenue was sprung to good effect. The impact of the anti-tank rounds' direct hit rocked the Swedish UN armoured personnel carrier on its chassis, the gunner seriously wounded died later of his injuries. Having been called to a conference of UN Unit Commanders and Staff Officers at UN Command HQ, Dogra Castle, the APC was transporting the officers commanding the Swedish, Indian and two newly arrived Ethiopian battalions and their respective battalion commanders, both Irish battalion commanders (the handover still in progress), and selected staff officers of the various UN battalions. Its occupants were badly shaken but as the APC was not disabled, it limped to UN Command HQ, only for them to come under heavy mortar fire mid-afternoon. In all, approximately 106 rounds fell on the area. Nevertheless, the conference continued in the cellar. For the return journey four APCs were provided to avoid this rich target presenting itself again in one vehicle. In the event this convoy too was ambushed by a company of gendarmerie. This time, however, there were no casualties and the four APCs drove smartly through.

With ongoing sniper and mortar fire on Irish and Swedish camps, the briefing had laid out that the requirement now of the UN, but particularly the Irish and Swedish, was to push out and enlarge their respective battalion perimeters and so their camp defences.

A combined operation was planned to expand the UN control of the Elisabethville area in a direction towards the city-centre but short of the tunnel proper. From intercepts it was learned that a major attack on both the Irish and Swedish camps was imminent that day, but Swedish and Irish mortars went into action on targets at the tunnel as later intercepts revealed that gendarmerie were 'weakened and becoming discouraged'. The attack never developed.

The night of 9 December was a nerve-racking nightmare for the Irish as the gendarmerie and mercenary mortars and machine guns kept up a continuous concentration of fires all night long on the Irish camp including harrowing fire from a Greyhound APC. Most mortar rounds fell short but there were some 20 that didn't. The troops spent the night again in their trenches and at this stage most had anything upwards of a foot of water in them. Contrary to expectations, no one was injured. From further intercepts it was learned that the gendarmerie were re-forming once again for an attack on the Irish camp. Irish mortars went into action, successfully. Again, the attack did not happen. There was a serious shortage of mortar and anti-tank weapons at this stage as 36th Battalion supplies had been flown to Albertville, their original destination. Over the coming days however, these armaments and ammunitions began to arrive in Elisabethville. For now, the Irish reply to attack was by measured means, content in the knowledge that the following morning would see a more offensive response.

The planned UN expansion operation towards the Liege crossroads, Point 'E', on which the Unit commanders and their staffs had been briefed, went into effect the following morning, 10 December, and was preceded by an air strike on the gendarmerie base, Camp Massard. Silver-coloured Swedish Saab fighter jets nicknamed 'flying barrels' because of their thick fuselage screamed in overhead, expertly piloted, while Indian Canberra bombers strafed other Katangan strong points. The UN now enjoyed air superiority and were applying it to good effect. The capture intact of 14 Katangese aircraft, the majority of their air assets, during operation Rampunch and the destruction of almost all the remainder during a crushing air raid on Kolwezi airstrip on 5 December substantially neutralised the threat from the air and the UN now pressed its advantage. As in almost all conflicts it is the ground forces, the 'boots on the ground' that have to actually secure the victory. It is this hard, tough, grinding out of on-the-ground fighting by the infantryman that ultimately secures, and importantly holds the objective and so the day. It is both deadly and dangerous and the issue at hand in Elisabethville was still far from being decided. Since Operation Morthor's unsuccessful conclusion the UN had been busy ferrying in materials and munitions, manpower and firepower; the build-up was nearing completion.

It takes a form of fatalism to put yourself in direct line of sight. Encouraged by the air-strike, nonetheless someone had to step out and be the ones first susceptible to a hailstorm of possible pinpoint accurate fire. Those advancing have the difficulty of doing so while concurrently responding to and/or avoiding defensive fire. The men of 'A' Company were without the advantage of surprise and neither shielded by darkness, nor screened by smoke. They knew all too well any prepared defences encountered must be suppressed before they were riddled by bullets and ripped apart from top to bottom by the immediate threat out in front, unseen, remaining hidden, no visible exterior sign of presence. There is neither mood music nor a dramatic musical score, nor an enemy that either convivially pops up or conveniently dies, and only a split second between being victor or victim. There is only one thing worse than wondering if someone out there is going to try to kill you, and that is *knowing* it. You can't *not* be afraid; the survival instinct is too strong.

This extreme exposure to fear makes you become very aware of the basic elements of self; the tension between having to be in the situation and not wanting to be; the strain of moving forward towards danger wishing instead to turn back and stay in safety; the struggle for courage, lost and found in one moment. Every man feels it, not many show it, all share it. But how to deal with it? The drill of cover and movement and if in the event of coming under attack is 'fire and movement'.

An infantry company has three platoons; each in turn comprises three sections. The ten-man section is the basic manoeuvre unit and this can be broken into two, one covering the movement of the other, leapfrogging forward ready to give mutual close-range supporting fire to the other, providing an ordered continuity of interlocking fire and movement. Good in theory, practiced in training, rehearsed in exercises; add the distinct element of fear to cope with and does it work for real? 'A' Company was about to find out.

Corporal Gerald Francis, the lead section commander of the lead platoon, Number One Platoon, recalled his unenvied task as a daunting undertaking:

I knew this was going to be difficult because the avenue along which we had to advance was an open road and we were highly exposed to being fired on. In the open we were going to be very vulnerable. I was highly conscious of the high probability of being fired on first. Chance and circumstance dictated it was me and I was all too aware of the potential dangers and wondered how best to deal with them. Glancing to my left as we advanced early on I noticed, looking down a connecting side road, the Swedes advancing along on a parallel route with APCs. As they advanced their APCs were pouring 'anticipatory fires' from their twin box-fed Madsen machine guns into anywhere in advance of them they felt attackers may be lurking so I raised my Carl Gustav submachine gun to my shoulder and did likewise and was quickly joined by the Vickers machine gun fires from the two Ford armoured cars. By means then of this 'active defence' while hugely exposed on the move was how we proceeded, hoping to seize the initiative from any would-be attackers, nullifying their advantage. That there wasn't anyone there or those that were decided the better of taking us on, the net effect was us reaching Liege crossroads without being fired on. The Swedes on the left route, us on the right route, Point 'E' between us.

The Irish battalion perimeter was now extended along Kasenga and Savonniers as far as Liege. 'B' Company had earlier cleared from the Police Camp (see map) to the beginnings of Rue De Kasenga whereupon the Swedes continued. Lieutenant Kiely had been injured by small arms fire. If the firing along the parallel routes had not provoked a direct response from the gendarmerie then it was because they were only waiting to do so by indirect mortar fires. The 'danger from the sky' was to rain down for days. Mortar fire is deadly. Its lethality deriving not so much from its explosive effect, unless it was an unlikely but possible direct hit, rather from the splicing slivers of fragmenting shrapnel subsequent to the shredding of its outer metallic casing on impact, around a killing radius of 25–50m. The larger the calibre, the greater the killing zone. Mortar bombs are fired – more correctly launched – indirectly, that is not in a straight direct line of sight from firer to target, instead lobbed from a firing line onto a target area, up and over in an indirect flight path following an arch-like trajectory. Mortars themselves are essentially metal tubes with a fixed firing pin inside at its base, the desired direction and distance governed by the angle of elevation at which it is set thereby controlling the fall of shot. The mortar bomb or round is slid down the tube, its base striking the fixed firing pin and projected skywards, the tailfin keeping its direction in flight steady and true. Individual pin-point precision is not required due to the dispersive nature of its deadly debris. Accuracy, especially over distance, can however be hampered by poor use of the weapon, varying wind direction, or fluctuating wind strengths, and so can cause mortar bombs to fall short, long or wide. Some fall on or near the target area but do not explode. These 'blinds' need careful consideration because they could yet explode themselves or if inadvertently disturbed. There is also a potential danger in the firing, that in a rapid fire situation a mortar bomb is slid down the tube and does not explode, then the firers thinking it has exited drop a subsequent mortar bomb down, which on contact with the one already in it explodes, this is known as a 'double-feed'.

An indirect fire support weapon's main use is to suppress enemy movement in defence or attack, to subdue their activities, to keep in check their advance, or ability to lay down defensive fires, or otherwise to 'fix' them in a position while one's own troops manoeuvre in the advance. 'Harassing fires' – intermittent indiscriminate firing onto a fixed position – can achieve the hoped-for demoralisation of an enemy. Underpinning all this, their main use is to kill, and to be on the receiving end of a mortar bombardment is not readily forgotten.

Fired singularly or in pairs, more often in groups, the more mortar bombs arriving onto a position, the more ground surface is covered, and so in this sense it is an area weapon. Such grouping of mortars causes them to be referred to collectively and conventionally as a battery, and their fires as mortar battery fires. Their use is not the sole preserve of any one side or the other, often mortar fires are used to respond to an enemy mortar firing line. Such 'counter battery' (CB) fires are conducted by mortars of equal calibre, these duels, however, frequently escalated in the number of mortars employed and use of higher calibre ones for more impact at longer ranges. Because they are fired indirectly, concealed from the enemy's observation, a Mobile Fire Controller (MFC) or 'spotter' gives directions and adjustments of the fall of shot onto the target. For him to do so he has to have direct line of sight onto the target, to see the rounds' impact, how near, far, or wide, and communications with the mortar firing line, to call in the adjustments. Spotting the enemy spotter's likely position and neutralising him is a way of disrupting the process and makes his job a hazardous one.

Significantly, Liege crossroads was in Irish hands and those gendarmerie accustomed to occupying certain houses from which they opened fire on the Irish camp got a hot reception when they found the houses occupied by the Irish at last light and fled under a hail of fire. Infuriated by the loss of Liege crossroads a very severe mortar barrage was placed on the Irish positions during the night. Irish mortars replied. Approximately 105 mortar bombs fell throughout the area. Trooper Sheridan and Corporal Ferguson received shrapnel wounds and Corporal Gorman received a bullet wound; three more added to 'A' Company's casualty roll.

The following day, 11 December, Point 'E', Liege crossroads, came under heavy mortar fire again. The determined barrage impacts sent dirt flying in a wealth of noise and smoke and sucked the air out of the atmosphere; the combined effect being highly disorienting, causing those on the receiving end to feel highly debilitated. The danger causes a panicked scramble for cover, to get behind something, anything, to get some object, layer, structure between you and it; every second urgent as it might be your last, shelter always seeming too far off; your dugout not deep enough, its top-cover not nearly sufficiently protective. Shouting, curses, heart thumping madly 'thud, bang' after 'thud, bang' after 'thud, bang' then silence, an acute silence, a momentary dizzy yet very deep silence, the only disturbance your own thought that surely no one else could have survived that. But is it actually over? You stir tentatively. Is it only a lull, will a misfire explode belatedly? You strain to hear the tell-tale whistle of further incoming. Nothing heard, you peer around, your weapon close at hand. Amongst the barrage six direct hits alone on Point 'E'.

Amid the menacing mayhem there were lighter moments as well; Lieutenant Sean Norton describes one such:

We were dug-in defending a strategic cross-roads, with our HQ 200m to the rear. An hour before sunset, we were subject to a mortar-bomb attack in the form of a creeping barrage, moving from front to rear. As the bombs came nearer the HQ, the personnel there were ordered to their trenches.

The first man to reach the large trench at the end of the garden was the head cook. As he was about to jump in he stopped suddenly at the entrance. This caused the others behind him to form a very agitated queue. By now the bombs were ripping-up the adjoining garden fences, showering them with debris. Everybody shouted 'Jump In', to which he replied 'I can't, there's a f***ing frog in it'. Needless to remark, he was dumped head first in on top of the hapless frog, with his comrades in on top of him.

The moral? It is not always the obvious that frightens.

Inevitably, accompanying small arms fire poured in from the area of the tunnel itself and south of Avenue Kasenga. Captain McIntyre 'B' Company received a bullet wound, his platoon assisting 'A' Company. Irish mortars replyed.

At Liege crossroads by day three, 12 December – over 48 hours since its commencement – attrition began to take effect, the constant wearing down of stamina, weakening of nerve, wrecking resolve; these and more are called into question as the weariness seeps into the senses. This is where self-belief, confidence and concentration are required and four times during the night Commandant Fitzpatrick, Company Commander of 'A' Company, called for mortar support fires to break up gendarmerie concentrations in forward positions. Inevitably, Katangese mortars replied and incredibly, unmercifully, unimaginably, Sergeant Paddy Mulcahy was wounded again for an unlikely second time, twice in five days, tragically; injuries he was to die from four days later. Privates Woodcock, Desmond and Confrey also took shrapnel wounds during these mortar fires.

At last light, in order to neutralise Katangese mortar fires Irish battalion mortars put a heavy barrage down on Katangese positions. Notwithstanding, intermittent mortar fire fell on all Irish positions during the night. These mortar positions were successfully located and fired on by the Irish. The confrontations during day three were not confined to mortar duels alone –

these ongoing exchanges of indirect mortar battery fires and counter battery fires – but also direct small arms encounters with Katangese and vehicles. M8 Greyhound armoured cars and 'Willys' jeeps with all their combined associated armament – 37mm cannon, .3 and .5 calibre HMGs thrown in for good measure – advanced towards Point 'E' and with grim determination were driven off by accurate fire from 'A' Company positions. Though hard pressed at times they kept up sustained fire putting rounds back in the direction of the attackers who disengaged. 'A' Company were now well and truly 'blooded'. Under attack on arrival and under constant fire since, Corporal Fallon killed and five wounded on day one, the advance and holding of Point 'E' was to see Sergeant Mulcahy die of his wounds and nine other assorted casualties from a mix of mortar and small arms fire, all sustained within a week. 'A' Company had received their baptism of fire which was to be further forged on the crucible that Point 'E' was turning out to be. They were proving silently heroic and resilient in the face of fierce hostility. There are many types of courage and different degrees of bravery, all in essence derived in the overcoming of felt fear. You do not have to have a weapon in your hand to display it; your actions are intended to help others, not to gain personal recognition. This was recognised in a number of instances where individual selfless acts ordinary in themselves but extraordinary in the time, place and circumstances performed, that in their execution inspired or at least encouraged others and in this regard were significant. Injured Private Woodcock – despite his wounds and obviously in pain

– vulnerable and uncertain of his prognosis, remained calm and urged that other casualties receive medical attention before him. Private James Fallon – brother of Corporal Michael Fallon – despite his brother's death on day one insisted on remaining with the company in theatre when it was easily understandable that he return to Ireland. Sergeant Paddy Mulcahy – injured once – refused to leave his platoon and returned to his duties only to put himself at risk again looking after his men and unfortunately paid a heavy price. Private James Murray, in tirelessly supplying food to those in exposed positions and even after having one container blown clean out of his hands by a mortar bomb, continued to maintain an appreciated supply of cooked meals. Corporal Charlie Connolly – regardless of his safety – as a medical orderly attended casualties under heavy mortar and small arms fire continuing to bring medical aid to the wounded, despite the danger involved.

With the UN force fighting for freedom of movement, the capacity of the Katangese to provoke was not yet exhausted and they set up a further roadblock near the large Socopetrol petrol and oil depot on Avenue Usoke in order to secure fuel supplies for themselves and to cut off the Irish and Swedish camps from UN Headquarters. Commandant Pat Quinlan, his namesake Lieutenant Tom Quinlan, and elements of their company of Jadotville Siege fame, within days of being homeward-bound were once again pressed into action and having passed through defensive fire penetrated close to the depot and set a number of storage tanks ablaze with offensive fire. Not satisfied that all the tanks had been destroyed he again approached the depot, this time commando style. He and his squad infiltrated through a swamp, at times up to their waists and even necks in water to set the remaining much-needed fuel tanks ablaze. Flames were rising to an estimated 300 feet lighting up the countryside and causing some concern at the airport, five miles to the northwest, because of the nightly bombing raids. However, no bombing was attempted on that night and the blaze continued for four more days. This hampered Katangese motor movement for awhile.

The Katangese still retained a bombing capacity under the direction of mercenary pilot Jerry Puren. A South African, he had World War II service in bombers with the South African Air Force and later flew transport planes with the Royal Air Force seeing service during the Berlin airlift. Recruited as a mercenary in 1961, for the next seven years he was intensely involved firstly as a mercenary on the ground and then an air commander, and later as an aide to Tshombe himself. Initially paid $1,000 a month, he became one of the very few mercenaries fighting in Congo for the Katanga ideal not solely for the money. The early involvements saw his planes strike against Baluba concentrations, dispersing the Jeunesse warriors along northern borders of Katanga around Lake Upemba and Kabala; later attacking ANC troops of the Central Congolese Government crossing Katanga's border from Leopoldville and Stanleyville mostly. Now having held a few planes safe from the UN jet fighter attacks on Kolwazi airstrip by holding them in nearby but much smaller airstrips he was both conducting and directing night attacks on the UNs Elisabethville airport. He flew a converted Dove aircraft used as an eight-seater transport or for light cargo deliveries. By rigging a rack system along the interior fuselage to take bombs of 12.5kg payload, making a hatch in the floor, and putting a plastic bomb sight thrusting up from the floor, the Dove aircraft became modified as a bomber. By pulling a lever bombs were dispatched one at a time through the hatch in the floor. By such means he in his Dove, together with two Dornier aircraft, the Katangese responded at night to the daytime raids by the UN jets. Thankfully, for the most part their aim was largely inaccurate. But those below were not to know until after the fact.

During the next two days (13 and 14 December) heavy mortaring onto all Irish positions continued. Some of this counter battery fire responding to Swedish mortars firing from 'A' Company's locality. Captain Harry Agnew was injured, losing one and a half fingers to shrapnel slivers. At one stage during these heavy exchanges it was requested by the American Embassy that mortar fire from Irish lines should stop to allow the evacuation of 500 women and children from the Athene schools. This was agreed to.

The identification of Katangese mortar positions was vital in the ebb and flow of the ongoing exchanges which rapidly developed into duels. After three days and three nights of almost continuous exposure to heavy incoming mortar barrages a very definite direction was given whose aim was to determine exactly where the location of the enemy mortars were. It was imperative they were found and neutralised. This involved the mortar OP (Observation Post with the MFC) going to higher ground. To do so necessitated crossing a road under constant bombardment and having to move the necessary radio equipment, a C-12 Wireless, a heavy large cumbersome set in itself but also two large 6V encased 'wet' batteries to power it. This required the crossing over of the exposed road no fewer than four occasions all the while under fire. The observers, Paddy Guerin and the previously injured Paul Ferguson, now gave a new 'fire mission' order with revised directions. The first fall of shot was declared 'near', the second 'on' — remarkable. Thereafter the enemy mortar line was taken out by 'A' Company counter battery fires. A lot of damage was inflicted, neutralizing the gendarmerie. This took a lot of unwanted 'attention' away from the Irish positions along Liege crossroads, now the secured spring-board from which to set up the advance on the tunnel.

On one subsequent occasion the sighting of a gendarmerie Greyhound armoured car in a firing position behind a house in Belair — a residential area for white settlers South of Avenue De Kasenga — led to the further discovery of new mortar positions also located there. Surrounded as they were by city residents, the Irish could not direct fire onto them; the Katangese were taking full advantage of any opportunity afforded in the circumstances. Any such advantage was very short-lived however as these exchanges were about to be rapidly overtaken by events and happenings dictated by the UN Force Commander; Operation UNOKAT was about to be put into effect.

10

Seize and Hold

'A' COMPANY'S ARRIVAL INTO CONGO AND THE BUILD up to Operation UNOKAT had been, in terms of time, barely a week but in terms of experience it had been an electric escalation. They arrived as tentative peacekeepers, had to immediately become tough peace-enforcers and would soon be tantamount to 'war fighters'. This tacit transformation from timidity through tenacity to temerity had been torrid and traumatic, the journey taut and tense, both brutal and bewildering. Shot-up on touchdown, subjected to several attacks since, under constant mortar and sniper fire, they had been heavily pounded for the last four days. Having sustained one fatality and suffered several seriously wounded, they were no longer raw; far from being green. They had gone through something monumental which had been intense, fast and fluid. Being 'new to the fight' there was an excitement and drama to it, but this was neither history nor Hollywood, all too authentic and pressurised, the close combat degenerating. They were beginning to get ground down, their tempo degraded, their energy sapped, already they were tired. The situation demanded a step up in toughness; they had to go toe-to-toe with an 'enemy'. The undertaking of a military conventional offensive operation was now the task in hand. The taking-on of this manoeuvre had associated tactics and techniques, trained for, but now for real. A full blown deliberate company in attack, part of a battalion action, itself a portion of the plan involving a brigade formation operation, was the challenge to be accomplished with the added specific consideration that it was to be conducted in darkness and within the urban environment of Elisabethville. Fighting in built-up areas is difficult, lengthy, and more costly in terms of ammunition and also, potentially, casualties.

The tunnel, a vital railway bridge intersection with a dual carriageway underpass, controlled a crucial avenue of approach access into central Elisabethville; it was a key point from which to continue the attack and support future operations. The gendarmerie under mercenary supervision had the time, means and weaponry to prepare and fortify selected key point buildings and structures as strong-points; the tunnel itself ideal for this purpose. The string of bolstered up buildings, improved protected positions, mutually supporting, were certain to offer stiff resistance. A defence of this type due to its nature is more easily able to withstand assault. An attacker faced with fighting in a built-up area will immediately look first and formostly to bypass; next to neutralize, stand-off and fire-in; to destroy by artillery, tank or air bombardment; and only as a last and least favoured option to conduct an assault. The tunnel area was the centre of gravity of the Katangese defence of Elisabethville; it was on this that everything depended and 'A' Company had to rupture it. Bypassing or reducing it to rubble were not options, the tunnel had to be seized and held the hard way. It was boots-on-the ground, troops-on-the tunnel time.

A crucial bottleneck, the tunnel was the single access

point, the vital valve controlling the flow to and from the city centre from the south as for approximately 2km either side was built-up completely. It was a critical choke point of strategic importance. To seize requires advance, advance demands forward movement, movement needs impetus, maintaining impetus under fire is dependent on momentum. It is difficult to keep the continuous tempo of an attack after you have been fired on at close range. The inclination is to remain in cover and from there return fire. Junior leaders have to push hard. Despite training and instruction the tendency is for men to bunch, to misuse ground and cover; this has to be fought against throughout an action. The success of an attack operation in particular depends on the initiative, energy and determination of junior leaders in applying the company commander's plan. Giving effect to this offensive spirit is fundamental to getting and keeping men moving towards seizing the opportunities and gaining the objective. When soldiers come under fire they want reassurance, want direction. The moral strength of the commanders as much as the physical means available is what really gives effect to planned actions. The most important weapon in any war, however, is intelligence and the UN didn't do intelligence, yet it was effectively at war.

It was very evident the task that lay ahead for the Irish was not going to be easily achieved. There are many things that militated against such efficiency, some controllable, others not. Knowing the ground, particularly the terrain whereupon sits and surrounds the objective is important. 'A' Company were without proper maps providing indication of the nature of the ground or buildings on the objective. Air photographs were not provided. Organic fire support weapons – those within the company 60mm mortars and medium machine guns – were in short supply, radio communications poor. But every commander at every level knows you cannot possibly hope to possess all the advantages all of the time, the reality of the situation you are faced with is often far from the text book theory ideal. Notwithstanding, the requirement remains, the objective has to be taken, the mission achieved. What was a given was that the Katangese Gendarmerie were now a well-equipped force which had grown more determined. They were well-led by battle-hardened, experienced, ruthless mercenaries who were a thinking adversary with a well conceived campaign plan. Up until this operation they had been going from strength to strength and implementing this plan granted them a direction towards success. It began with harassing tactics with close-in firing on UN camps at the time when the Irish and Swedish Battalions were rotating. Their aim was the confinement of these raw new Battalions to their camps. Next, to isolate them from their supply line; in this they were almost successful to-date; the Irish, Swedish, Ethiopian and Indian Battalions were denied routes Alpha and Bravo through Elisabethville. Finally, to seize the airport thus denying the UN its strategic APOD (Air Point of Disembarkation) and base.

UN command therefore had to counter and a plan to implement the destruction of Katangese resistance in the Elisabethville area was hatched; Operation UNOKAT was born. A brigade in attack with a further brigade encirclement; in effect a division-sized operation would be launched. The operation to be carried out in two phases. Phase one was to contain and keep pressure on the Katangese Gendarmeriés and mercenaries, in the tunnel area particularly, with mortar fires pre- H-Hour (the exact time for the attack to commence). Phase two, the investment or surrounding of the city by the Indian and Ethiopian Battalions by cutting off and blocking key routes – effectively sealing the city – preparatory to the destruction of the Katangese Gendarmerie and mercenary resistance in the Elisabethville area by the Irish and Swedish battalions. This second phase was itself made up of two parts, one for the Irish 36th Battalion, the second for the composite 12/14th Swedish Battalion. The one brigade-sized manoeuvre involved two deliberate and deep battalion-in-attacks – one Irish, one Swedish – supported by Indian 120mm heavy-mortars. The specific mission for the Irish Battalion falling out from the brigade operation order was the vital tasking to seize and hold the tunnel and to exploit forward thereof in order to secure the right flank of the Swedish attack on the gendarmerie Camp Massad. The UN brigade-in-attack plan for this offensive operation had therefore to synchronise the efforts of a number of elements of different nationalities, to co-ordinate their moving parts with fire support, properly integrated to a precise timetable, in order to dominate the fluid tactical situation. Falling out from this the individual battalion staffs, each in turn, prepared their respective attack plans integrating with the specific detail of the brigade's mission and its coordinating instructions. Thus was 'Operation Sarsfield' brought into being, with

'A' and 'B' companies the main attack on respective twin axes, mutually supporting with 'C' Company minus in reserve. The main effort of the entire brigade attack and overall divisional effort lay in the hands of the Irish, and as circumstances were to play out, hinged mostly on 'A' Company's efforts to seize the tunnel. In addition to its significant tactical importance, its capture would have immense psychological value, smashing the Katangese grip on the city's access, the UN retaking control of its freedom of movement and the overall situation. In exerting its military force in support of its mandated stand the UN was making a massive statement to the world that it was prepared to back its position militarily. The loss of this major junction was crucial in breaking the morale and will of the gendarmerie and the mercenaries. This was high stakes stuff, tactically and strategically, both militarily and politically. It would be heavily defended and not easily given up. The importance of the plan, its clear communication, and effective execution was emphasised at the 'O' Group; this is where the commander imparts his plan to his subordinates through the issue of orders. These full formal verbal orders are the key to ensuring that commanders within the battalion clearly understand the part they have to play in the upcoming action; that all important aspects are covered; a precise prescribed formatted sequence is followed; that the mission completion is paramount is emphasised, the mission itself stated unambiguously, then restated for effect. Questions are answered and no effort spared to ensure a clear understanding of the coordinated action to conduct the operation is arrived at. More than that the commander will press his personality on the operation and motivate his commanders verbally. It is here leadership, that unseen but immediately obvious quality, comes directly into play and the unit cohesiveness of action is built around the commander's intent, and Lieutenant Colonel's Hogan's intent was very clear: the tunnel was to be seized and held, and 'A' Company were to do it.

11

Codeword 'Sarsfield'

Operation UNOKAT

IN THE AFTERNOON OF 15 DECEMBER 1961 LIEUTENANT Colonel Michael Hogan Officer Commanding 36th Infantry Battalion received orders for the UN offensive to commence early the following morning (16 December). He issued orders at 9.00pm; H-hour for the attack to commence on the tunnel was fixed for 4.00am. In the intervening hours between receiving his mission and issuing his own orders Lieutenant Colonel Hogan had to prepare his plan of action and his unit for combat. In the circumstances, time was the number one enemy and he had to know both what, and perhaps more importantly, *how* to think in order not to allow precious hours and minutes slip by. Having been given his mission he now had to prepare his plan to achieve it, and these efforts would only culminate when having estimated the situation he was tasked with he would develop and impart this plan via his 'O' Group (orders group) and launch the troops of his battalion across the start line as fully prepared as he possibly could make them into the forthcoming fray. To craft his plan he had to consider what the mission accomplishment tasked him with, both stated and inferred. What had he, in terms of military assets available to achieve it, did he need additional support, and how was he to organise all of this to best effect. In the given circumstances he and his staff had to determine the risks associated with the various options in light of the successful accomplishment of the essential tasks required of him and decide which were acceptable. Military men do not gamble, they take risks, but they do weigh the different degrees of risks between one course of action and another. Mentally, methodically war gaming and scoring each. When it comes to analysing the mission the trained military mindset works backwards, so to speak. A reverse logic and mental process kicks in, beginning with the objective to be achieved, then an analysis of the time and physical manoeuvre space available to achieve it, in order to establish the correctly sequenced chain of events to be set in motion. This then drove the schedule of activities that had to occur. Out of this process fell clarity, the more concise construct of the essential mission for the 36th Battalion plan, its precise purposes and specific tasks.

There is an old army saying that 'time spent on reconnaissance is time well spent'. An initial 'map recce' is conducted, also consulted are any available air photographs if to hand. This informs the undertaking of the on-the-ground physical reconnaissance, important in the assessment of terrain and developing the courses of action. The advantages and disadvantages of each course of action are considered and compared and a decision arrived at. In this case the maps were of limited use, there were no air photographs and the physical reconnaissance restricted so as not to give the game away to any observant gendarme or mercenary. It was nonetheless useful in confirming the obstacles that would slow the advance, disrupt the movement and impede the manoeuvre to the objective; the tunnel. It was a built-up area, highly suited to defence, there were open spaces good for the defender's observation and fields of fire, bad for own troops cover and concealment, and of course the gendarmerie and mercenary defenders held the key terrain, that which held key advantage and upon whose capture the entire mission hinged. Consideration of the tunnel defender's situation would try to identify how they were physically positioned on and near the objective, where were his strong-points and of what strength was he composed with what equipment. What were his capabilities, to avoid; his weaknesses, to exploit? Lieutenant Colonel Hogan and his staff brainstormed the alternative options, seeking a preference. They asked themselves if tasked to defend the tunnel how might they organise it. Finally, he gave consideration to his own troops. They were for the most part seasoned, sound, non-commissioned officers (corporals and sergeants) and young – many very young – privates, most inexperienced, certainly ill-prepared for what had confronted them thus far and what now faced them. Still not recovered from the lengthy journey from Ireland, the apprehension of strange new surroundings was debilitating in itself allied to the general air of nervousness, concern, tension and stress of the continued hostilities; the discomfort of no beds and snatching a few hours of sleep all had a huge wearing down effect on their physical and mental energy. However, they'd had exposure to the many experiences of the almost non-stop series of incidents since arrival during the build-up and this plan Lieutenant Colonel Hogan knew would make a difference, a big difference, rather than attempting the undertaking without having any. They were well and truly 'blooded', some amongst them not gung-ho exactly, but after enduring the retaliatory mortar fires inflicted on them for days at Liege crossroads – some in storm drains with water up to chest height and with casualties suffered – were keen to have a go.

The second battle of Katanga was well and truly underway. Since 5 December it had marked a new deadly phase to the conflict. The UN was stunned by the loss of life resulting and now its on-the-ground lines of communications were being slowly strangled; its competence and commitment challenged; its operation's very existence threatened. Forcefully facing up to this adversity presented the opportunity for the UN to get on the front foot. Operation UNOKAT would close the UN net around Elisabethville. Operation Sarsfield would see the Irish, as part of Operation UNOKAT, go after the high value target that was the tunnel, the immediately adjacent railroad and the hospital complexes. Operation Sarsfield was about to commence. They deployed expecting a fight, and a fight was what they were about to get.

12

'A' Company Action

WITH LIVE ROUNDS OF AMMUNITION IN THEIR weapons, the seconds and minutes ticked down. A live 'enemy' out in front with live rounds of ammunition ready to fire at them, 'A' Company was poised to become involved in large-scale live action. A lot of moving parts had already been set in motion. The codeword 'Sarsfield' for the Irish attack to commence had yet to be transmitted by the battalion commander. The men of 'A' and 'B' Companies were to move across staggered start lines, their parallel axis of advance along the railway line and Avenue Des Savoniers, respectively. 'A' company were to advance with numbers Two and One Platoons forward left and right, Commandant Joe Fitzpatrick in the centre, Number Three Platoon rear right and the Company HQ under Captain Kevin Page rear left. Already ahead of them and forward left were 'B' Company. 'C' Company minus moving behind in reserve. Both 'A' and 'B' Companies had already sustained casualties during the week since their arrival. The men were worn down, weary but not yet fully exhausted, and despite their tiredness were in good spirits. Nonetheless, when out beyond the point of no return, having crossed their start lines, understandably each would individually be contemplating the now inevitable fight and so were apprehensive – some terrified – yet all ready to face the difficulties, enduring the strain, but all definitely on edge, unease and concern palpable. Theirs' was an ability to control this fear and suppress its effects, this in a word, was courage. Commandant 'Bill' Callaghan (later Lieutenant General and Force Commander of UNIFIL 1981 – 1986) then OC of 'B' Company explained:

The night of the battalion orders – the evening before the attack on the tunnel – in the battalion headquarters at Leopold Farm, there was evident a tension and an anxiety, and afterwards I remember saying to myself somewhat understatedly, 'I hope this goes well'. Nonetheless there was also a feeling that we had been given a job and that job we were going to do, we had a shared objective, but different parallel axes of advance.

Interestingly, initially these were reversed to what transpired, as later the respective axes were changed to ironically facilitate the thought-to-be less difficult approach to be given to 'A' Company after their harrowing experiences at Liege crossroads over the recent days. 'B' Company were now tasked to approach head-on along Avenue des Savoniers and up along, forward of triangle FGD (see map), with 'A' Company right-flanking along the railway tracks. After the battalion orders each company commander held his own 'O' Group to disseminate the battalion Plan of Attack, Commander's Intent and Scheme of Manoeuvre, and their specific part in its achievement. Second Lieutenant Peter Feely (later Colonel) was platoon commander Number Three Platoon of 'A' Company:

The night before the attack on the tunnel I felt afraid of course but not an overwhelming sense of dread or anything like that. Since our arrival the weather, the new and strange surroundings, the unfamiliar noises at night, had all generated a sort of nervousness, but over the eight or nine days and the episodes building up to the attack on the tunnel you quickly learned to recognise what was of immediate, obvious and urgent risk, and that was what became of concern to you. However that night, the 15 December, after the company commander's orders and briefing, prior to getting a few hours sleep I shared a can of Guinness with Lieutenant Paddy Riordan. Having opened it we both took a few small sips only, each leaving the majority of the can's content unconsumed, whereas ordinarily both would easily have accounted for it, so perhaps there was an unconscious concern and muted fear. Overall, however, I felt a definite overriding sense of relief. Relief that we were no longer, after the experiences of Liege Cross Roads, continuing to sit and get hit-up, rather going on the attack, getting up, moving and doing.

Lieutenant (later Colonel) Sean Norton, Platoon Commander Number Two Platoon 'A' Company put it another way:

On the 'start line' on 16 December, for the attack on the tunnel it was pitch black and the rain was bucketing down. If I didn't feel afraid I'd be afraid of myself. Every leader must have fear; it keeps a discipline in your thinking. For the most part however I was concentrating on what I had to do, getting on with the job in hand, my responsibilities took up my thoughts and my thinking.

During the form-up on the start line (SL) numbers One and Two Platoons had to exchange places as they had got into each others form-up positions by mistake. This was a second such fateful chance readjustment that future circumstances would later play a tragic hand in. On the upside, the UN force now enjoyed air superiority, with most of the Katangese aircraft captured or destroyed. News of the successful UN air strike on Kolwazi airstrip on 5 December was greeted by a furious Tshombe who had been in Paris; his enraged reaction expressed the unambiguous statement that this could now only mean 'real war'. Following the mercenary led gendarmerie actions since, real war was what was now resulting in the sense that the UN Operation UNOKAT was a conventional-style military-type undertaking. The weather was both a hindrance and a help; the torrential rain hindered control and movement of the Irish advance, but at the same time along with the pre-dawn darkness helped to cover their movement. It was also a hindrance insofar as the advantage of air superiority was wiped out, the planes unable to take to the air or identify safely their targets, a help in that it sheltered the approach of the Irish adding to the cover provided by the darkness.

The synchronised pre-H-Hour mortar barrages had commenced with firing in advance of 'B' Company's earlier crossing of their start line. The orchestration of this 'mortar music' was conducted by laid-down timings in the Brigade Fire Plan, its gradual but ever-building tempo rising to a cacophonous crescendo as the mortar fires engaged their specific target areas concurrently ahead of the choreographed movement of the UN troops' advance. The Indian 120mm heavy mortars 'lifting and shifting' fires, first in front, then to the rear of the tunnel area. These fires adhered to the strict detail of the scheduled scheme of the laid-down fire plan, thereafter available 'on call'. A fire plan is the synchronised target-specific, time co-ordinated use of the effects of the artillery, mortar, and air assets available to fix an enemy in position and/or force them to seek cover while ones' own troops advance (in relative safety). Such on call fires were necessary to react to unanticipated situations arising as difficulties and different circumstances developed and their effects necessary to counter any mortar responses from the Katangese and mercenaries. As more and more mortars reigned in on the opposition positions, there was movement, much concurrent movement. The UN, overcoming its difficulty in getting reorganised since Operation Morthor, having previously struggled to get a purchase on a peacefully negotiated political platform, refused to be bullied, and having traded punches with the Katangese was now taking the full blown firefight to the secessionists mercenary-led force. Keyed-up UN soldiers from the Indian and two Ethiopian battalions moved first to surround and seal the city before the Irish and Swedish stormed in. This initial encirclement was to isolate the Katangese forces, the city's investment preventing them being reinforced, providing direct fire support for own UN forces, and protecting the assaulting troops from counter-attack. Their adrenaline triumphant over trepidation, the Indian Ghurkhas and Ethiopians moved out commencing the 'surround and storm' objectives of Operation UNOKAT. The Indians moved east and north, the Ethiopians west at Lido. A number of clashes occurred with the Ethiopians fighting fiercely, losing 14 dead, with four wounded; the Indians had one fatality. The battle had begun, the Indians and Ethiopians playing their part; next up were the Irish.

Operation Sarsfield
The Battle of the Tunnel
(16 December 1961)

13

Advance to Contact

WE WERE READY AND 'ON' TARGET FOR THE TUNNEL.
We had found our ranges beforehand the previous day,
recorded them and also the line with two aiming posts.
I knew what I had to do, but had never done it before;
firing overhead, with moving troops underneath, for
real, was a big responsibility for someone with limited
experience. Sergeant Joe Scott, Sergeant Michael Butler
and Corporal Paddy Guerin were 'A' Company's main
'mortar men'. They, Private John Woolley, and others
in support of the platoon marshalled the gun line,
consisting of three 81mm mortars. For his part John had
joined up, underage, the previous year for excitement,
and with the possibility of UN service in Congo
materialising had volunteered along with everyone else
for the 33rd Battalion. He recalls his experience:

*I actually got picked but was dropped off the list because
my mother wrote in to say I was underage. I was furious
and disappointed. Private Joe Fitzpatrick replaced me. He
was with those who were involved in the Niemba ambush,
one of only two survivors of the eleven-man Irish patrol ...
would I have been* [a survivor]? *I went out with the next
battalion, the 34th, which was an enjoyable experience
for me, so I went out again with the 36th Battalion.
Busy on arrival, we were firing day and night for seven
days. Because it was the wet season in Africa there was
a lot of mud around; inevitably, no matter how careful*

we were, sometimes some of the mortar bombs got dirty and damaged. Also 'fouling' built up in the mortar barrel and occasionally mortar bombs got stuck in the mortar tube barrel. Once we spotted a mortar being set up by the Katangese and received orders to fire on it, first shot was reported back as 'near', second shot as 'nearer', third shot as 'hit'. So now 'on' for distance and direction we dropped a mortar bomb into the tube, it got stuck, we cleared it and dropped a second bomb in, it too got stuck. As this was happening, the 'enemy' mortar crew got up and ran away — they'll never know how lucky they were.

In all, during that week prior to the attack on the tunnel, the outgoing number of mortar rounds we fired came close to a thousand. The crews used to put extra charges (relays) on the mortar fin, kept in place with rubber bands, to get extra range. Extensive use then of a weapon, the general attitude towards which, scarcely a week before, was that it was never going to be fired; after all, we were going on a peacekeeping mission.

Sergeant Michael Butler recalled:

When digging the mortar trench I was myself guilty of something that I so often before gave out to students on courses and soldiers on exercises for not doing: digging a 'sump' in the pit itself, so, in case it rained, the water would flow off the bottom of the trench into it. On the early morning of the 16 December it rained heavily and in the downpour we began, as per the fire plan, firing at [2.30am], other firers had commenced at [2.00am]. On the early morning of the 16 [December] there was a

'A' Company 84mm anti-tank training in 'The Glen' prior to departure to Congo.

The aftermath.

Dug in at Liege crossroads.

Captured mercenary weapons.

Aerial view of the tunnel.

Coffins homeward bound.

Corporal John Power.

Corporal Mick Fallon

Holding the bridge.

Lieutenant Paddy Riordan, DSM.

Private Andy Wickham.

Inspecting the damage.

Mortar position, tunnel.

Mortared outhouse (Cpl Mick Fallon RIP).

Sergeant Paddy Mulcahy, DSM.

Shot-up aircraft engine.

'Re-org'.

*ONUC Force Commander & UN Special
Representative, Katanga.*

Refugee camp.

Refugees arriving.

prolonged monsoon-type torrential downpour. The mortar trench became sodden very quickly, so when we fired the first 'warmer' round out of the mortar it got embedded in muck and we had to dig it out. The mortar fire plan tasked 36th Battalion mortars to commence, continue at a given rate of fire, then cease, at specific times and targets. The muck was making this difficult and at one stage Private John Wolley's mortar had gone so far down in the pit the sights were below the level where it was possible to use them. So he took the barrel off the base plate, threw sand-bags onto the base-plate and parts of his uniform, then placed the base plate from one of the other mortars on top, then the barrel, and recommenced firing maintaining the 'rate' of fires required. Once we were finished we were soaked with rain and filthy with mud, but the job was done, the Fire Plan completed.

Neither were the Irish the only ones adversely affected by the heavy rains because as 'B' Company advanced up along Avenue des Savoniers in full frontal view of the tunnel – although some distance away – they encountered little resistance. Surprised, and needless to say relieved, they did notice a number of shallow dug trenches well-filled with rain as they progressed along. It occurred to them the gendarmerie must not have taken too kindly to the weather and sought shelter in the railway carriages further back. Consequently they were not encountering any resistance and were not being held up. All the while heavy mortar fires overhead were suppressing and weakening the defences on the tunnel itself and subsequently any defensive positions in depth (not linear or shallow, rather extending rearwards).

The overall plan of attack was dependent on the operation's tempo, the UN force's speed of activity relative to that of the opposition's, aided by its audacity, the willingness of the attackers to take risks, and both rapidity and boldness — the weather conditions fortuitously favoured their delivery. However the Irish were well aware, whatever the weather, that the gendarmerie and mercenaries were not going to simply give up the tunnel. It would have to be seized from them. The tunnel was the decisive point of their defence and so would be heavily defended. They could not ride on their luck forever and surprise alone would not carry the day. At some point the Irish knew it would take a dramatic and determined drive to wrestle it from them. The strong points would have to be stormed.

Ready to advance, 'A' Company had, however, to move forward on a very narrow frontage. The configuration of the urban man-made topography of the built-up environment meant that instead of the convenient, conventional, clear parallel axis for mutual support between their lead platoons in line, they were canalised, channelled and confined to moving on either side of the railway tracks in two columns each. Designated one behind the other on the left-hand side of the railway tracks, initially Numbers One and Two Platoons had found themselves formed up incorrectly in each other's place. This had to be rectified, with all the noise and clatter that two groups each of 32 men plus some attachments, with all their equipment, trading places would generate. Fortunately the downpour covered the noise, the darkness, the visible movement, the distance, the commotion from carrying forward. Fifty years later, retired Colonel Sean Norton DSM, then a lieutenant and platoon commander of Number Two Platoon remains struck by the irony of what subsequently developed, ensuing to what at the time seemed an innocuous, inconsequential, almost unnecessary correction. In the event, he was not to dwell on it because Commandant Joe Fitzpatrick Officer Commanding 'A' Company ordered them across the start line; 'A' Company were now on the offensive. They moved out as one; sombre, serious and silent. The fighting not yet begun, inwardly each was already at war with himself, struggling with the situation and faced with the demands of upcoming combat, not knowing if he was a match for it. The advent of going into action had the strong but at the same time strange quality of being stomach-churningly tense while also presenting a heightened sense of excitement. They were under no glorified illusions, any misapprehensions had been shattered since arrival. Their short service in Katanga to date had been physically demanding and hugely stressful. In the attack proper they knew speed would be crucial. The maintaining of momentum and movement, critical. Commandant Joe Fitzpatrick and each of his platoon commanders, Lieutenants Paddy Riordan, Sean Norton and Peter Feely, in charge of Numbers One, Two and Three Platoons respectively, understood this. Looking for the muzzle-flashes of any would-be snipers, anticipating ambushes, negotiating and clearing obstacles, maintaining silence, ensuring no one got lost, coping with the weather and the darkness degraded the speed of progress and prolonged the duration of the approach. Corporal Gerald Francis, point man for the advance, rememebers:

I guided the section and so the platoon and hence the entire company right at Liege crossroads along Avenue Liege. Forward left of us 'B' Company had already reached and secured the area known as triangle GFD where the roads Chaussee de Kasanga and Avenue des Savonniers met. The forward point or tip of this triangle faced the tunnel at a distance of some two hundred to three hundred yards which was directly in front of them further along Chaussee de Kasanga. For my part, where Avenue Liege met the railway tracks at the level crossing, I opened the gate and the platoon, with the remainder of the company following, swung left onto the railway tracks, which were parallel to Avenue des Savonniers. Completely dark and lashing rain we advanced up along the railway tracks. The distance of the gap between the wooden railway sleepers underneath and supporting the railway tracks did not correspond to the length of a normal mans stride and so we walked, quietly along the side of the tracks, knowing this would lead us directly in onto the tunnel from the right. All we had to do now was follow the tracks and not alert any sentries.

A penetration more than a flanking envelopment, the sheer boldness of the frontal manoeuvre hinged on stealth and getting as close to the tunnel as possible before being spotted. 'A' Company needed to be methodical and synchronised, clinical and determined, but first and foremost, forward and concentrated in order to achieve surprise. They knew their actions, reactions, and presence of mind on 'contact' needed to result in the rupturing of the defenders' resolve to resist; they would have to be forced into giving up the tunnel. It was a clash of wits and wills, a battle of nerves as much a test of war-fighting skills. Crucially they had first to gain a foothold to launch the assault proper. Commandant Joe Fitzpatrick knew what had to occur to make this happen. But before this he also knew the time was surely nearing when they must come under hostile fire. There is a saying amongst the military that 'the best laid plans rarely survive contact with the enemy', a saying he was hoping not to be true on this occasion. Each step nearer the objective without contact was borrowed time, however. 'A' Company, prior to departure to Congo had trained hard in the Glen of Imaal, County Wicklow to be able to perform well that which they hoped they would not have to. Four weeks later, they had crossed an actual start line and were advancing to contact, for real.

14

Contact

THE CONCERTED TWO-PRONGED APPROACH WAS progressing well, in the case of 'B' Company's a little too well. Lieutenant Tommy Dunne, commanding the point platoon of 'B' Company, was out in front. He remembers:

It was pouring rain and quite dark and I was aware only of going in the general direction of the tunnel until suddenly we found ourselves in a dip in the roadway. Sergeant Enright, Platoon Sergeant, gasped audibly realising where we were, 'Sir', he said, 'the tunnel, we're almost in it.'

The dip in the roadway was the gradual downward slope of the dual-carriageway underpass beneath the railway line tunnel itself. Concurrently, on their right 'A' Company were at their most exposed approaching within the last hundred metres or so of the tunnel proper. Corporal Gerald Francis Lead Section Commander Number One Section, Number One Platoon, 'A' Company, recalls:

We followed the tracks all the way along and it brought us to within fifty yards, almost on top of the tunnel. We were so close we could hear the gendarmerie talking. They had put on the tunnel itself two railway carriages and had placed themselves in them along the parapet of the tunnel. We stopped at an agreed point and it was here the company was to get into – as much as space allowed –

an 'Arrow-Head' formation. Lieutenant Riordan and his radioman Private Andy Wickham went forward beyond me. Suddenly a blast of gunfire, I think from one of the railway carriages on the tunnel, was directed our way. Lieutenant Riordan fell and didn't move. I kept looking at him to see if he would move but he didn't. I had to be sure he was dead. I was in a kind of disbelief. The survival instinct is a very strong one however and it took over. They were not firing at us as specific individual targets, they were blasting away in our general direction, aiming I would say on fixed lines impacting on the walls of the buildings behind us. Their ammunition was arranged in many of the weapons in use against us in a sequence of armoured piercing, ball and then tracer. So every third shot of the incoming rounds were tracer and such was their volume I remember seeing the luminous, glowing, melting phosphorous from these dripping down the walls around us. It was at these impacts that other firers now placed their aim. Our platoon had hit the ground, Numbers Two and Three Platoons were strung out along the railway track behind us, moving immediately sideways off the railway tracks into cover.

Though inevitable, it was nonetheless sudden, sharp and shocking in its occurrence; an edgy, raw, alarming, menacing violence. Although braced for it, the contact when it came was unbelievably brutal, causing that involuntary individual full-body freeze-frame, a shivering shudder, and then the momentary mental registering of the realisation 'this was it', all occurring within a split second. The shots shattered the suspended atmosphere, projecting 'A' Company into a whole other sphere of activity, one of urgent reaction. The bullets ripped through the darkness with a pulverising potency and tore into the night, shredding any illusions of an easy victory. The firing, not pinpoint accurate, nonetheless had a reckless intensity, an improbably heavy volume and a murderous intent. Number One Platoon took the full ferocity of the first fiercesome fusillade. Be it design or chance, it was Number One Platoon's commander who was downed. Reasoned or random, Lieutenant Paddy Riordan fell, fatally wounded. The loss of its commander at this critical moment threw the platoon into disorder, a disarray further degraded by the ongoing pummelling being put out by the voracious defensive screen.

When fire was opened on them Number Two Platoon under Lieutenant Sean Norton went to ground on the left, taking cover in the welcome folds and undulations of an open space. They were pinned down by the ever increasing rate of incoming fire from light, medium and heavy machine guns and an increasing, undetermined number of riflemen. When fired on in such volume at close quarters the natural reaction is to go to ground and stay there. The most basic instinct is to remain as you are while the bullets whiz overhead and impact around you. The earth is your friend, shielding you from harm. It is entirely counter-intuitive to want to move. You are safe where you are. Both conscious and unconscious reasoning compels you to stay stuck to the ground, that is until your platoon or section commander orders you to move. Even then your sixth – survival – sense pervades upon you not to budge one inch. For all the urgings of someone else, be they in command or not, there is a marked reluctance to move. In order to survive the ever-increasing volume of incoming fire Lieutenant Norton needed his platoon to move, and move now, though they felt they needed to stay.

Another scenario was developing forward on the railway tracks with Number One Platoon. Matters were more complicated and compounded there without their platoon commander, and their location in the more direct immediate vicinity to the source of the firing, still in the killing area. Cover, but cover from fire, not just cover from view was required. Lieutenant Norton knew he had to get something solid between his platoon and the enemy. The difficulty of control increased and the dangerous urgency of the moment became more apparent. For his part, before his platoon's reluctance to move became refusal, Lieutenant Norton resolved he simply was not going to allow his men remain where they were, and like a man possessed his drive drove them up, his 'get up and go' got them up and to the safety of a secure structure behind a disused, non-functioning hospital building. Every infantryman knows the soldier's mantra when encountering effective enemy fire. The basic battle drill of fire, dash, down, crawl, cover, observe and fire is the reaction rehearsed time and time again in training; 'for real' however, heavy bursts of incoming fire impacting close can cause the collapsing of your composure, can be a real challenge to your character, and from a command and control perspective can make things go fundamentally wrong. With his Number Two Platoon making for the safety of the hospital building led by Lieutenant Norton, Number Three Platoon in cover to the rear under the charge of Lieutenant Feely, OC 'A' Company Commander Joe Fitzpatrick knew he needed to get up to Number One Platoon to regain its shape, otherwise they could be ripped apart by the incoming fire, horrific in it's intensity, and all too soon be in free-fall, powerless to resist and be unable to address the momentum. To rectify these issues in the heat of battle requires a special kind of mindset.

Meanwhile at the forefront of 'B' Company's advance Lieutenant Tommy Dunne had halted his platoon and moved his two sections into buildings left and right of the road, the third into a shop they subsequently called 'Dunnes Stores' in the apex of the road junction FGD, facing the tunnel. Moving with his platoon runner Private Mick Daly, while checking on his sections' locations they came under fire from the gendarmerie defenders along the tunnel. As they ran for cover they accidentally tripped over an unexploded rocket shell, fired previously during the week from a UN jet fighter, embedded upright in the middle of the roadway. They landed one on top of the other in a helpless, hopeless, haphazard heap; a happy landing as it happened because had they not fallen where and when they did and remained fully upright a savage burst of heavy machine gun fire would have cut them to pieces. The Irish were now well and truly about to become involved in a full-on fire-fight.

15

Fire-fight

THE QUICK-FIRE EXPLOSIVE BARRAGE OF BULLETS was like a whirlwind sweeping all before it. It was unrestrained ferocity with a decidedly mean streak of malevolence intended. This was a full-throttle hammering delivered by automatic weapons in the hands of people who knew how to sight and use them to great effect. The Irish advance was hurting and in trouble. They were under intense scrutiny and all their suppressed fear was coming to the surface. The defenders had steam up and were surging ahead, pouring out a furious rate of fire that was full-on and fast; anything and anyone exposed would be blown to smithereens like matchwood. Before their will wilted and they retreated in a rabble, their quest quickly quelled then quenched like the throwing of a switch, Commandant Joe Fitzpatrick knew he had to immediately reconfigure and get a structure back into his shocked, stalled and stricken lead platoon. Operation Sarsfield comprised the requirement to achieve surprise followed by the winning of a short, sharp engagement. Putting this into effect, 'A' Company had been on the cusp of completing almost total surprise, when to their surprise, once discovered, the resulting contact was so fierce that it had thrown its lead platoon into disorder. If such disarray was allowed to degenerate further it could completely dissolve the company's momentum, disintegrating the attack's initiative completely. In being tasked to take the tunnel, 'A' Company now had a mountain to climb. Commandant Joe Fitzpatrick with his lead platoon stricken, his platoons separated, his company pinned down, communications made difficult by a lack of radio sets and their poor range and effectiveness, the initial contact costly in fatalities and injuries, and heavy fires continuing to pour in, had somehow to reignite the impetus of the advance. At that point in time, the mountain ahead seemed like Everest but he was in a conquering frame of mind knowing 'A' Company's primary battle was within themselves, each man having to find in himself that desire to succeed. He had to turn their individual doubt into a collective sense of self-belief. He had to make fighters of the frightened.

To have a fighting chance, Lieutenant Sean Norton knew they had to cause events to happen faster than the defenders could react to them. He knew the intent of his company commander's orders and in turn the goal of the battalion commander's. This he felt was not going to happen by standing still behind cover; instead he had to achieve this goal by dealing with what was happening there in front of him. The consequence of the decentralised nature of how the advance had evolved granted him a freedom of independent action but also placed upon him an onus to identify and seize any opportunity presenting itself or to make one happen. Suspending the reality of the shock of the situation they found themselves in, undoubtedly a very tight spot, he needed some clarity of thought. Further bursts of gunfire from the tunnel gave him his answer: simple things work best, they were going to blast their way back into the battle. If nothing else it would surely lift spirits. This stark, ruthless, cold-blooded resolve was to be the catalyst for their revival; they were going to win the fire-fight and pave the way forward for a turnaround. They were going to stand-up and fight. More correctly, kneel down and fight, with the 84mm anti-tank recoilless rifles perched on their shoulders.

Developed to be used in a defence setting in a conventional war-type scenario to cover the main tank threat, in this case it was a versatile, multipurpose, direct fire resource under the command of the battalion commander. It had an identified offensive use: to secure the advancing battalion's assembly area, forming-up point and start line and later in the attack the final assault against enemy armour, then finally the reorganisation position against counterattack. Highly adaptable and flexible, its use could adjust specifically to the task to be undertaken and so was organised to be given to the appropriate sub-unit, consistent with the particular role for which it was intended to be deployed. So it was that 'A' Company were given six, two per platoon, with a view to their aggressive use, and so placed well forward under close control of the platoon commanders. These proved lighter, more portable and quicker into action than the light 60mm mortar used by platoons. In any case, 'A' Company only had one 60mm mortar and were similarly short of light machine guns. In terms of support fire weapons available within the platoons, the anti-tank recoilless rifles were it, and it was up to the platoon commanders to make use and take full advantage of them. As far as Lieutenant Sean Norton was concerned they could well have a pronounced impact and be the answer to their stiffest test, causing the hunters on the tunnel to become the hunted. 'A' Company were bloodied but not bowed. Put to proper use the resulting blast impacts on the tunnel's parapet could well have the deterrent effect on the gendarmerie and mercenaries and a galvanising one of recovery and resurgence for the Irish, energising them, Lazarus-like. The shock of the Katangese response would have to be turned into the awe of an Irish reaction. The face of war may have changed dramatically but it is still the deadly primal collision of wills between opponents.

'A' Company had identified that the 'eighty-four' had the potential to grant a perceived and real edge if used correctly. They had trained and practised with it in 'the Glen' previously, firing it repeatedly at traversing tank-shaped cardboard cut-out targets and had admired its effects. New to the Irish army, their predecessors the 35th Battalion were the first to bring it into service overseas. A number of promising 'shots' had emerged and one such was now entrusted with the task of 'taking out' the firepower focused against them.

The battle was soon set to be joined; its close quarter combat between the Irish attackers and the Katangese defenders about to become aggressively engaged. The gendarmerie and mercenaries had employed a judicious mix of machine guns and a high density of individual riflemen spread along the parapet of the tunnel's railway bridge, amongst railway buildings and inside railway carriages. The railway bridge parapet in particular provided ready-made, instant cover.

Running full-length over the entire width of the dual-carriageway underneath along the railway bridge itself was this walled parapet set on its external edge, a ready-made concreted 'balcony' even in its original form, but both barricaded and fortified proved ideal and was a strong-point in itself. This key man-made feature was a structure affording excellent fields of fire and a hugely advantageous defensive position, except that is, for what Lieutenant Sean Norton had in mind.

There was a difficulty with their plan, however, as considerable risk was involved. A characteristic of firing the 'eighty-four' anti-tank weapon was its significant signature back-blast of flame exiting from the rear of the gun, necessitating back clearance when firing. A direct-fire weapon using line of sight to the target required the firer and his number two to have to step out from behind the safety of the cover of the disused hospital building, remaining exposed to the heavy automatic fire. If the machine-gunners reacted quickly enough the firer would surely be mowed down even before he got his shot off. There had to be a readiness then to face and endure this definite danger, to struggle hard to suppress this fear. There was a high liability and a possibility of harm or death.

This then was a particular moment to put yourself in a perilous, precarious position and leave matters to providence. Pressed hard against the cover of the hospital building, intensely aware of the circumstances, all too conscious of the possible consequences, were you going to manage to step out, however momentarily, or not? It was will over wisdom and single-mindedness over sense. Was it to be payoff for those painstaking days, weeks, months of training and years of preparation? It had all come down to this. Suddenly courage won over caution, fatalism over fear, as with a slight lull in the firing he stepped out, knelt down, placed the loaded 'eighty-four' on his shoulder and picked out a machine gun position along the parapet. Hands starting to shake, weapon wavering – *steady, steady* – he takes in gulps of air, oxygenates the brain, settles down, picks out his target again, squeezes the trigger and lets loose the anti-tank round. The roar of its ignition erupted, the brilliance of the flamed flash of brightness from its back-blast dramatically lit up the still pre-dawn darkness, only to be superseded seconds later by the noise of the explosive detonation of its impact on target. The defenders had one less machine gun. The Irish had a foothold on the fire-fight.

16

Men Against Fire

'THE IRISH WERE BRUISED, NOT BROKEN' WAS THE message sent and delivered by the impacting 84mm anti-tank round; the thrust of the attack, though stalled, was not breached. Concurrently, further stemming the tide was Corporal Gerald Francis perilously perched at the point of the hapless lead platoon. Notwithstanding, he readily risked exposure to rally those immediately around him and opened up returning fire with his Gustav sub-machine gun at the left-hand side railway carriage. The firing from it stopped, only to commence again. He instantly returned fire. This exchange happened in the same manner three more times. He was conscious that he was shaking, and taking stock of himself made a deliberate effort to intentionally calm down. In doing so he somehow remembered that the characteristic of the Gustav sub-machine gun is that when fired on automatic with the finger constantly squeezing the trigger, the rounds arch upwards to the right. Thinking it to be both curious and timely to recall this he proceeded to fire single shots only, one after another in quick succession and used a full magazine of 36 shots in this manner. The firing from the carriage ceased. He then engaged the second railway carriage and Private Andy Wickham joined in, the pair to be joined a little later by Private Gerry Kelly and Private Michael Searson. Being the furthest forward, the four together as a group tackled the defenders from the right, keeping up solid volleys of intensive return fires. All this took time to unfold and as it was happening Number Two Platoon under Lieutenant Norton were developing their own situation. Meanwhile further left, staring point-blank at the tunnel Lieutenant Tommy Dunne's platoon were not idle. Back on the railway tracks Corporal Francis' small group were now fully and decisively engaged in an intense fire-fight. Despite their valiant efforts, the Katangese delivered a murderously heavy volley and in its wake Private Andy Wickham fell injured; Charlie Connolly, the medic, got to him, but despite his attentions and persistent attempts to render first aid, his wounds proved fatal. Corporal Francis now called on his 84mm anti-tank team to attempt to respond and engage those ahead. He selected the left-hand railway carriage as the target and instructed the use of an anti-personnel round at minimum range aimed seven feet above the roof. Calling back that the group would all be within the danger area nonetheless in the heat of the moment Corporal Francis instructed them to do it anyway. They did. It worked perfectly. They were instructed to repeat the dose. Number Three Platoon further back under Lieutenant Peter Feely had manoeuvred into firing positions and when they spotted movement amongst the railway carriages, they engaged. Such individual exchanges were happening simultaneously, many mini-encounters occurring within the consternation. Back with Corporal Gerald Francis, his section had two 'energas' with it; an FN rifle with a fitting or attachment on it allowing it to fire energa grenades. By pushing in a special round it fired off a projectile that looked like a rocket-shaped, grenade-type device, the advantage being it would travel further than if thrown ordinarily, hence greater range achieved. He fired; it hit the second railway carriage but failed to explode. Not put off by this he got ready the second one and as it happened a gendarme appeared with rifle raised so he fired directly at him; this one worked.

The Irish were holding their own. It was a definite improvement on where they had been, but they were still not getting to where they needed to go. As the intensity of the exchanges grew Private Gerry Kelly sustained a serious gunshot wound to the groin, and other casualties were being taken. The firefight was in the balance. There was enough edge and steel in this compelling clash that each side believed they had the greater imperative to prevail; the Katangese defenders in no mood to capitulate, the Irish unrelenting in attack. One elemental force had to give. Defending with all their guile and know-how, if able to sustain their rate of fire the gendarmerie and mercenaries could maintain dominance. The status quo was not going to achieve the mission for the Irish; they could all too easily become forestalled and so simply had to force a change in their fortune somehow, but how? Meanwhile Private Christy Lynch, a radioman to Lieutenant Sean Norton heard the bad news over his radio, 'two down at Number One Platoon.'

17

Fire for Effect

WHEN THE HUGE WEIGHT OF KATANGESE FIRES ERUPTED, lost Irish initiative resulted. Even though many shots were being fired blindly through the darkness at them, their sheer volume was a considerable deterrent to movement. The Irish predicament was acute. Now well forward they were exposed and vulnerable. The attack stalled, the onset of brightness was progressing, and the tactical balance of the situation would further favour the defenders as come daylight they would be better able to clearly see what they were shooting at. Frayed nerves, already raw and tense, could easily prove their undoing.

As he looked anxiously out across the ground in front of the tunnel, taking cover from the withering firing, Lieutenant Norton knew the attack hung in the balance. A bad situation was getting worse literally by the minute. He also knew when faced with a seriously deteriorating situation you have to do something about it. A capacity to invent ideas, to use every tool you have, to cause a process to begin was badly needed. Lieutenant Norton was determined the Katangese triumph would be short lived. The key to breaking a strong defensive position is to find a soft spot, then exploit it. There really wasn't any but the success of letting loose the 84mm anti-tank round suggested to him an increased concentration of this firepower at the crucial point could be decisive. Events needed to be dramatically influenced and Lieutenant Sean Norton, encouraged by the firing and effect of the 84mm anti-tank round wanted a repetition. But, discouraged by the improbability of survival, urged caution. Lieutenant Norton vividly recalls the moment:

> *Given that we had achieved success the first time, I felt a repeat of the same was in order. It was best under the circumstances to accompany the firer this time and so we both stood out together; he fired and found his target, two machine guns silenced. We ventured out seeking a third hit and found it. Three rounds in all, three hits. The intensity of their fires waned somewhat.*

Tenacity won out over terror. Simultaneous 84mm anti-tank round impacts onto the tunnel parapet and into the railway carriages under the direction of Corporal Gerald Francis, and from neighbouring 'B' Company's forward position under the direction of Lieutenant Tommy Dunne all creating a critical moment, but only if seized upon. The battle itself was in the balance. This was the break-through moment for the break-in. Lieutenant Sean Norton recognised it, and trusting his instincts ran forward, as if possessed, into the unknown. His platoon, no more knowledgeable about what exactly was out in front of them, followed, exploiting their opportunity, willingly grasping it, keen to reinforce success, even keener to do whatever it took to stop being fired at.

18

Impact

ALONG THE TUNNEL'S PARAPET, FROM INSIDE THE railway carriages and the railway yard's buildings, the gendarmerie and mercenaries had kept up an inferno of flying lead at the Irish. In the darkness amongst the noise, their excitement, and the rain, they first saw the blinding flash of the 84mm anti-tank gun's backblast then heard the roar of its ignition overtaken seconds later by the thunderclap explosive detonation against the tunnel's parapet. The strike's eruption had an instantaneous, abrupt shock effect. The projectile's forceful collision with the rim of the tunnel, a shuddering impact, took out one machine gun and caused the others to immediately fall silent.

The tunnel's defenders were shocked. Seconds later they were showered with clumps of charred concrete, the billowing smoke choking, and impact noise still ringing in their ears. Their cessation was only momentary, however. Urged on by the mercenaries, they resumed their ferocious, blistering, radical rate of fire at the Irish. That is until the second 84mm anti-tank shot resulted in a second hit, followed shortly by a third, causing consternation. Pandemonium followed when the air burst detonations from Number One Platoon's 'eighty-four' added to the chaos whilst the fires from 'B' Company's created a combined lethality from which they could not recover, as the severity of the concentrated 84mm anti-tank fire was sustained, crippling and destructive. There was no viable response. The defenders were overwhelmed and overwrought; their resolve to resist was rendered rapidly redundant. The persistence of the explosive collision of the anti-tank rounds smashing repeatedly against the parapet's concrete caused a massive maelstrom of mangled masonry which forced the defenders to flee.

19

Break-in

MISTAKES HAPPEN IN WAR. 'BLUE ON BLUE' SITUATIONS occur when you come under fire from other friendly own forces mistaking yours for the enemy or vice versa. Amongst the doubt, fear, darkness, miscommunications, the movement, strain, speed of happenings, confusion, the 'fog of war' errors, often a combination of small individual mistakes occurring simultaneously, have consequences, sometimes fatal, for one's own side. A fired-up Number Two Platoon 'A' Company under Lieutenant Sean Norton, bouncing back from the brink of being seriously shot-up, now energised, were on the move. It had seemed like the Irish advance could have collapsed in the face of the sudden, severe, exceptionally heavy fires. It had been a moment for serious soldiers to stand up and be counted, and they had. Having survived the first 'unfriendly' fire, an horrendous, harrowing hostility, to now fall victim to 'friendly' fires would be tragic in the extreme, and this all too easily could have happened with Number Two Platoon 'A' Company emerging from the right, straight across into 'B' Company's arc of fire to their front. Number Two Platoon's advance took them from behind the cover of the disused hospital building, down the embankment onto the dual carriageway, across Chaussee des Kasanga and up the other side into the railway marshalling yard, taking fire all the time from the tunnel area. Private Pat Lally, born in Mellows Barracks, Renmore, Galway, whose family members before him had seen generations of soldiering with both the Irish and British armies recounts the event:

I was tall and lean so maybe that was why I got the Bren gun (light machine gun of World War II vintage which fired .303 calibre ammunition. The LMG provides the main fire-power for a section, of which there were three in a platoon). It, together with the magazine boxes of ammunition were heavy to carry. Having been fired on, then taking cover behind the hospital and advancing towards the railway yard, we had first to cross the dual carriageway with the weapons, ammunition, backpack and poncho. Moving over a fence I fell head first, ending up with my feet pointing skywards, unable to move, up-ended. Someone behind me pushed my legs forward and I was able to gather myself. I remember, along with others, firing a number of bursts into the railway carriages where fire was being directed at us, and the firing stopped.

The shock action of the 'eighty-four' blast-effects dislodged the defenders from their laterally arranged strong-point. The Irish having got in close by stealth, meant they were upon them, their defence shallow, lacking depth. Their reaction when it came, however, was frantic and ferocious from well set, well laid out support weapons firing along fixed lines into anticipated avenues of approach made convergent and restrictive by the built-up area around the vicinity of the tunnel, forcing the fight into confined spaces, making their fire more lethal and deadly. Abruptly halting the Irish advance, they turned its cohesion into confusion, the regaining of control further complicated by the darkness. The Irish fight back granted a chance of a possible purchase position as a basis for progressing the attack and Lieutenant Norton set about pressing this possible advantage.

By this stage Commandant Joe Fitzpatrick had drawn parallel to Corporal Gerald Francis and his half section, looking for a situation report and a casualty status. Pulling up a chain-link fence they scrambled underneath to meet up with him, continuing to give covering fire all the while at those who were firing on them. Corporal Francis at this stage had run out of ammunition so as the two men spoke Corporal Francis reloaded two 36-round magazines. Commandant Fitzpatrick's concern was to get the remainder of Number One Platoon off the railway tracks and into proper cover. Enquiring of Commandant Fitzpatrick what he and those five others from Number One Platoon's lead section who were with him ought do now, he was instructed to join the advance with Number Two Platoon. Corporal Francis was bleeding from his left ear lobe and Commandant Fitzpatrick was concerned for him, however as he was feeling no pain he did not feel like getting treatment at that stage. Commandant Fitzpatrick was keen to gain ground and have the company move forward beyond the railway carriages in case the Katangese Gendarmeriés and mercenaries were re-forming for a counter-attack. They were. Corporal Francis calls the moment to mind:

The Katangese Gendarmerie and mercenaries had

withdrawn from the tunnel's parapet but we were unsure, – and it was dangerous to assume – that they had vacated the railway carriages on it. So Lieutenant Norton took his platoon down onto the dual carriageway and up the other side into the railway station's marshalling yard. Now we were aware there were three large companies of Katangese gendarmerie in defence of the tunnel area (100 in each) and while we had bloodied them there must be plenty of others about. As it happened there were, and we were suddenly in amongst them.

There were stationary engines and railway carriages, there was darkness, shooting, shouting, confusion; the Irish attackers, hugely outnumbered, became intermingled with the Katangese defenders. It became a very chaotic affair, a shapeless frenetic effort, the Irish suddenly flooding in on a collision course; who was friend, who was foe; where was friend, where was foe; impossible to know what was happening beyond your very immediate surroundings; a situation ripe for 'blue on blue', survival an unpredictable outcome. After three or four manic minutes of mayhem and madness, the Katangese Gendarmerie panicked somewhat and withdrew. The instinct for survival dictates the Irish were not worried about those running away from them but far more concerned about anyone lingering, and that occupied their minds and actions. However, with the tunnel in their hands the Irish 'tails were up', morale was high, emotion taking over, and the platoon's advance became extended. Corporal Dan Mannix kept going with others, threatening to go beyond the safe distance of exploitation, risking running into the 'shifting' mortar fires from their own 81mm mortar section supporting the attack from Liege crossroads firing line. Checking themselves, before they became victims of their own success, they came back and those railway carriages in the marshalling yard allowed them some respite until fire began coming into them, whereupon they got out, went under these railway carriages, taking cover behind their steel wheels and returned fire. Lieutenant Norton described the advance:

Three rounds, three hits, the intensity of the defenders fire waned momentarily, sufficient to push the platoon forward and the further we went, curiously, the less resistance we got, so I kept going, exploiting the situation. We moved forward rapidly under the covering fire of four more 'eighty-four' rounds and so much so I was afraid of over-extending my advance and becoming cut-off or isolated. In the event, we did become a little stretched.

The situation was much improved, the tunnel was in Irish hands, however things were a long way from secure.

20

Assault and Clearance

IN CHARGE OF THE DEFENCE OF ELISABETHVILLE WAS the mercenary commander Colonel Roger Faulques, an ex-French Legion paratrooper, a veteran of Dien Bien Phu (Vietnam) and Algeria. From a sandbagged, camouflaged nerve-centre in the centre of the city he directed the defensive operations, commanding a necklace of key positions at vantage points all around the capital. These were a series of entrenchments, a ring of fortified structures manned by groups of Katangese gendarmerie led by mercenaries equipped with support weapons – carefully sighted machine guns mostly – all backed up by on-call mortar fires. Facially scarred and walking with a slight limp he had maintained command and control from his hidden headquarters, co-ordinating the main Katangese defensive effort. On a large bank of radio sets linked through individual frequencies to the front line strong-points and support elements he received the situation reports and incident updates, responding with instructions and orders. Ever more hard pressed, he was becoming increasingly concerned by the adversely developing situation at the tunnel.

Lieutenant Norton's platoon, having penetrated hard, had fought fast to gain a forward foothold. The two other platoons under Commandant Fitzpatrick's overall direction were now following, fighting forward also in quick succession. Fire was still pouring in on them, the matter not yet clear cut and much in the balance. There was plenty of fighting still left to do.

Lieutenant Norton was keen to make the most of the opportunity presenting but was fearful that where his advance paused it might remain, so he pressed the advantage while he had the upper hand, eventually culminating it himself before his platoon became too overstretched. They had progressed all the way from the cover of the hospital building down onto the dual carriageway, up the bank into the railway marshalling yards amid the momentary mix-up madness, then progressed in pockets well down along the railway tracks. Now they had to turn around, consolidate and clear. Inevitably, small unit actions broke out and followed as individual groups of reinforcing gendarmerie inexplicably stumbled headlong in from the side. The first such approach was a group of four in a taxi with windows down and weapons protruding, suddenly confronting a small group of unsuspecting Irish, each group baffled, disbelieving what they were seeing, both a split-second away from and a hair-trigger between, life or death. Whomsoever reacted quickest survived. Private Tom Foster's instincts were fastest, his wits keenest, his aim sharpest. Bringing his Bren gun into action, he brought a line of fire onto the vehicle and saved the day.

Having cleared the area in and around the big railway yard sheds, Number Two Platoon now turned their attention towards assaulting the railway station building proper. However, very heavy small arms fire began to be received from the PARC VT area (an adjacent commercial area to the railway yards); Colonel Roger Faulques was not conceding the tunnel just yet. One of the factors in the broader ongoing battle in the wider Elisabethville area was now directed to come into play: mobile fire bases. These jeep-mounted mercenaries equipped with .3 or .5 calibre vehicle-borne Browning heavy machine guns, recoilless rifles and bazookas, raced, under the direction of Colonel Faulques, to plug gaps, strengthen the resolve of wavering gendarmerie positions and stiffen the opposition towards wherever the advancing UN most threatened their defences. Job done in one location they moved speedily to where next directed and needed. One such mercenary jeep-load with a .5 HMG arrived and engaged Number Two Platoon who responded unhesitatingly, hitting one occupant, and the vehicle roared out of sight behind the railway station building. 'Dropping a section' as a fire base, where ten men put down covering fire, the remaining two sections of ten men each manoeuvred left-flanking onto the railway station building. The firing from this area dwindled as the attack progressed. On reaching the building the jeep had been driven away and somehow they knew it wasn't coming back any time soon. The platoon was then ordered to secure the ground held and an 'eighty-four' anti-tank weapon team were told to return back up along the railway yard to the tunnel area to deal with an outbreak of further firing emanating from the railway carriages on the tunnel itself. Two rounds silenced the firing. Two Gendarmes hurriedly jumped down from the railway carriages and made off up the road towards the roundabout.

In so doing they ran into the fire of Number Three Platoon under Lieutenant Feely who had been given responsibility to clear the area northwest of the tunnel. One month short of being promoted to full Lieutenant and getting his second 'bar' (or today a 'PIP' – rank insignia), Peter Feely's Number Three Platoon had next been ordered to clear the remaining unchecked railway carriages in the marshalling yard for hidden snipers and gendarmerie gunmen. This he set about doing himself with the use of Mills 36 hand-grenades, lobbing them through the windows before, once exploded, entering the carriages to clear them with his Gustav sub-machine fire. He describes it:

> *Approaching the first railway carriage I lobbed a grenade towards the open window only it fell short, bounced off the window frame and dropped onto the railway tracks; there it remained, without exploding. This wasn't supposed to happen, you were to pull the pin, throw, and it exploded, only I did, but it didn't; now what? Wait. Wait for it to go off, but when? After a moment or so I lost patience and moved, I felt, in fact I knew, I had to. It didn't explode. Sequentially, systematically I cleared those railway carriages and the platoon moved on to clear the area.*

In so doing, both from the railway carriages and the area in general, gendarmerie were flushed out and seen running off. Character and action held 'A' Company in good stead resulting in the pendulum of fortune swinging their way. The tunnel was theirs.

21

Three Green Flares

ARM OUTSTRETCHED SKYWARDS, COMMANDANT JOE Fitzpatrick Officer Commanding 'A' Company had an important task to perform. He had slid the first flare into the chamber of his very light pistol and now holding it aloft squeezed the trigger. Up, upwards it went, momentarily disappearing into the darkened rain-sodden sky, swallowed up by the grey murky bleakness before suddenly, spectacularly exploding in a profusion of green. He quickly repeated this action, twice more. Three green flares, the signal for 'tunnel taken', mission accomplished, job done. A hard ask and a tough task, it had taken an assertiveness, well-trained troops, and self-believing junior leaders to complete and achieve it. The plan had not survived contact with the enemy and unusual things had happened and kept happening. The physicality and intensity of the close-in combat was full-on. The exchanges, unsurprisingly, had a significant edge. But there's a beauty in simplicity and the combativeness, competence, and confidence of the Irish had a huge bearing on the outcome. The contact had begun badly but the resultant anger arising had an energy, and sustained by composure they never wavered and had the wit and imagination to know they just had to make things work. To survive the withering fires of the opening onslaught, endure the nightmare of the sustained intensity before they thrived, to come back; they knew they had to make a significant play and have the final say. This composure of the collective effort, this refusal to lose, however, was every bit as much about a number of individual acts of bravery, courage, leadership and resourcefulness which were significant in their execution and achievement, in emotionally draining, physically dangerous, hugely difficult and dire circumstances.

'A' Company had just been through a sharp, intense, unforgiving fire-fight whose outcome was unforeseeable, unforgiving, and liable to be won or lost at any number of given moments, and it wasn't over yet. Colonel Roger Faulques was planning to give it one more last desperate throw of the dice. At 7.45am, one and a quarter hours after its seizure by the Irish, Colonel Faulques, mercenary commander of Elisabethville's defence, ordered a massive mortar barrage to fall all around the tunnel area. Everything he had was thrown at them. He, like the good combat veteran he was, sensed unless he could move the Irish off the tunnel, its loss could cause a momentum shift in the high stakes battle for Katanga itself. The moment was now, the position here, not only vital tactically but hugely strategically and symbolically significant as its turnover to the UN would grant them a corridor to dominate the capital and so grant the view the UN force had grown in stature, willing and able to give effect militarily to back itself politically. As the Katangese mortars opened up to pound the newly taken prized position the Irish braced themselves, steadfastly refusing to be denied their victory and that of the UN's. The battle for the tunnel had been a battle within a battle.

The three green flares symbolising victory, tactically, for the Irish Battalion fortifying a belief in themselves, strategically for the UN, galvanising their political efforts militarily, and personally for the individual Irish participants, strengthened by a seam of submerged raw energy coming to the fore when questions were asked of them.

The battle for the tunnel was the battle for Elisabethville, which was the battle for Katanga, which was the key to the battle for the Congo.

22

Reorganisation

'HE WHO DEFENDS EVERYTHING, DEFENDS NOTHING.'
So said Frederick the Great. Consequently
36th Battalion held the ground taken on the
16 December with two companies; 'A' Company
concentrated on the tunnel and 'B' Company nearby
linking with the Swedes. While most UN units were
spread thin on the ground the Irish, who held the most
important ground, had the task of dominating their
immediate area. It was one thing to seize the tunnel, 'A'
Company had to now make sure they held onto it. To
do so they kept their defence compact. The attackers
became defenders. To ensure against an infiltration
or attempted recapture of the cleared objective by the
Katangese, 'A' Company prepared a close-in all round
defensive perimeter encircling the tunnel with Number
Two Platoon and half of Number One Platoon south,
in the vicinity of the railway sheds while Number Three
Platoon and the other half of Number One Platoon were
north, in the area of the railway yard and hospital.

Defences set, the 're-org' was a consolidation on the
seized objective involving the holding of ground around
the area taken, for a period. Initially at least they had a
chance to draw breath and begin to ponder on what had
just occurred. Any sense of victory however was severely
tempered by the loss of Lieutenant Paddy Riordan and
Private Andy Wickham. Lieutenant Norton states:

There was no emotion evident, we were tasked to take

ground, now to hold it; consequently there was a lot to attend to. We had two dead and some twenty or so wounded. Matters were business-like; we were mostly wondering for how long we would have to be here. Curiously, only then did it strike me, we had been in the same uniforms since arrival on the 6 [December], some ten days previously.

They were put into action straight out of the plane. It had been high drama from the off, a direct approach required. They were presented with a very different kind of challenge than they had anticipated when boarding the Globemasters in Dublin Airport. Different questions were asked of them than they thought would be the case and all of this at pace. They controlled what they could control and got on with matters, demonstrating a collective will not to come out second best until finally they had to demonstrate a sheer bloody-mindedness and to become full of attacking intent. When put on the back foot on contact they found themselves involved in a titanic exchange but had more desire for the fight; the greater will to win. The Irish needed it more than the mercenaries wanted it.

In the reorganisation position, section and platoon commanders as a routine drill check their personnel, their individual ammunition requirements, and their fitness for the future fight. This basic procedure was to throw up a number of interesting instances evidencing the true exposure to the deadly nature of the undertaking they had just come through. Corporal Sammy Gregan was to identify that his 'jaw felt sore'; upon examination it was discovered there was a bullet lodged in it. He was subsequently repatriated medically to Ireland and so missed serving out the remainder of the tour with the 36th Battalion. He returned to the Congo with the 37th Battalion and was the first off the plane to greet his homeward bound colleagues. Corporal Gerald Francis, already shot through the earlobe on taking off his backpack discovered bullet holes in it; his tea-mug had a bullet hole clear through it. Corporal John Power was to find that his Gustav sub-machine gun mechanism had become jammed and he was unable to pull the mechanism to the rear. Seeking assistance, an inspection showed his weapon had been hit and damaged by a bullet. The Irish had well and truly been in the line of fire; quite a few had narrow escapes, near misses and close calls.

Physical fitness for further fighting ascertained the company could only continue to do so if they had enough ammunition. Resupply is an essential task to undertake early on in the re-organisation position and Captain Quartermaster Harry Crowley and his 'Q' team set to the task, Signalman Peter Fields amongst them,

We set off in our resupply vehicle laden with ammunition boxes and ration packs. Shortly along Avenue des Savoniers we unexpectedly came under fire so immediately pulled over to the side and ran into a house with a garage attached. I dived into the garage and looking out the window saw a number of gendarmerie running between houses on the opposite side of the avenue. We returned fire. There was no further firing in our direction so after a duration we resumed our journey. Not long after but still short of the tunnel we were surprised to yet again come under fire. Stopping abruptly we took cover on the side of the road and returned fire, round for round; the firing stopped. No further interruption was experienced. We drove under the tunnel and reported to Commandant Joe Fitzpatrick who was busily supervising the 'digging-in' consolidation process in anticipation of an imminent reaction from the mercenaries and gendarmerie. 'A' Company didn't have to be told to dig deep and dig fast. Fortunate not to have suffered more casualties, they had little time to wallow in any 'what ifs' because the real concern now was to ready themselves for the inevitable incoming mortar bombardment that must surely arrive. It did. It was soon evident that the occupation of their hasty defensive positions needed to be more dispersed and they redeployed. They quickly set about it. Mid-afternoon they were glad they had, a second mortar barrage as intense as the first had to be withstood. The location of the firing was identified as being from the Union Minière complex; 36th Battalion mortars replied. In between the Katangese mortar bombardments, in fact shortly after the first, the Swedish battalion moved out across their start line and two hours later had breached the defences at Camp Massard. 'Storm-In' was completed. Meanwhile the Indian Ghurkha battalion completed their move along Avenue Churchill and reached Athene School. The two Ethiopian battalions, having cleared the Lido and Zoo area, moved towards Camp Massard to close the ring around the city; 'surround' was completed. Operation UNOKAT was completed, and successfully so. There were 18 UN dead and 21 seriously wounded. The UN had taken the initiative and seized the opportunity, the second Battle of Katanga now going their way. The Katangese response was confined to indirect mortar fires, falling this time onto the Swedish camp. The following day, early morning, Indian heavy mortars were moved into 'B' Company area to bring Katangese mortars within range; threat countered. They were moved further forward later in the day into the captured Camp Massard to quell incoming mortars landing there. Due to the dispositions of the UN's 1st and 2nd Brigade troops around the city of Elisabethville orders were issued for the strict control of mortar fire.

Matters remained unsettled throughout the 18 December, with many mortar bombs falling on the tunnel area; a third day of bombardment. Sniper firing continued during the day, also into the 36th Battalion area. Notwithstanding, the Battalion Ordnance Officer commenced the disposal of unexploded mortar bombs, including a 4.2 inch one of British manufacture amongst the company lines and battalion headquarters area.

The UN force commander and Brigadier Raja visited the Irish lines, congratulating them on the seizure of the tunnel. Meanwhile mopping up operations by the Ethiopians and Ghurkhas continued in Elisabethville. There was a Baluba threat to move into the city from the refuge camp. Those who succeeded in reaching the city engaged in some looting. The UN Brigade Headquarters set up a depot for the storage of confiscated loot. Finally, at last light the 36th Battalion was informed that the water system which had been cut off along with light and electric power shortly after the Irish seizure of the tunnel had been poisoned. In any event, rainwater had been used for all purposes since the mains were turned off on the morning of 16 December. Not all things falling from the skies were necessarily bad.

Unsure exactly where the notion fell from, Lieutenant Peter Feely found himself inspecting the depth of the blast effect impacts on the concrete parapet rim of the tunnel:

As regards the penetrative effect of the fire of the 84mm anti-tank round on impact, it was said to be twenty-one inches on concrete, and on measuring this after the attack it proved to be precisely correct. It was a good weapon to have and I was glad now to have it on the re-org.

While Lieutenant Peter Feely was wondering about the depths of impact of the 84mm anti-tank gun, Lieutenant Sean Norton wanted to solve a riddle of his own. He walked to within a few metres or so of the rail carriages on the tunnel and let loose a number of 9mm rounds from his Gustav sub-machine gun only to witness them bounce off the carriages' exterior. They had little or no penetrative effect, due to a combination of small calibre round and tough material used in the construction of the carriages. Meanwhile, Corporal Sammy Gregan, being stretchered away, the bullet still stuck in his jaw, was wondering also; and indeed was completely distracted from what was going on around. All he wanted to know was if those who had shot him had been accounted for, and indeed they had! Reassured, he only then relaxed.

23

Aftermath

PUT STRAIGHT INTO ACTION FROM THE OFF, THE company had a mix of very young soldiers, old soldiers and seasoned NCOs. These senior NCOs proved very steady and together with the old soldiers successfully settling the young privates in those early days. They all learned on the job and once 'digging in' (digging trenches) had commenced didn't have to be told twice to provide good overhead cover, early, as the remainder of the trench was being dug. Mortar fire was very frightening. Even though it too was deadly, direct small arms fire – and you frequently heard it passing through the leaves on the trees – just didn't have the same menace about it, but mortar fires were bad, they bothered Captain Harry Crowley particularly, and he was not alone in this. He was not involved in the attack on the tunnel proper as his role was resupply, of ammunition particularly, especially on the 're-org'. Commandant Joe Fitzpatrick, the company commander, was very steady, soldiers of the company liked him, and he had worked them hard in 'the Glen'. Once Number One Platoon was fired on and the attack's momentum stalled he got in amongst them and moved them on, maintaining the impetus. Lieutenant Sean Norton Platoon Commander Number Two Platoon was really in the thick of the action from arrival to the tunnel 're-org'.

There were others who displayed courageous actions, accurate fires, leadership, coolness and control and where disregard for personal safety was evident. 'A' Company had in truth distinguished themselves with honour, distinction and merit. They were tough, pragmatic and modest about it. They had been given a job to do and were determined to go about it. That it was of the nature it became resulted directly from the drastic change in the UN mandate earlier in February, a more coercive resolution authorising the use of force in accordance with Chapter Seven of the UN Charter, a significant step up from its 'Police role' of keeping the peace to which now they hoped to return. What is as remarkable as them doing what they did was their unpreparedness to do so; no combat experience, under-equipped, no training of a continuous, comprehensive, collective nature – it was 15 years since the 'Emergency' ended in 1946. An amazing action, all the more so because it simply had not been done before.

An action of this nature was unexpected and certainly so when Ireland decided to face up to its responsibilities as a member of the UN, seeing participation as an obligation as a UN member state. Following on from the consensus of the UN Security Council Resolution authorising the mission in the Congo, and responding favourably when asked to participate, Ireland regarded it as an opportunity to demonstrate its identity as a truly neutral peacekeeper, keen to secure its reputation of being an ideal peacekeeping nation. 'A' Company's action at the Battle of the Tunnel certainly contributed towards that. As did Irish pack rations. Irish pack rations for 21 days were taken to the Congo with the 36th Battalion. They were popular enough with the troops but more so with other contingents on the occasions when attached to the Irish for rations. They were superior to the American day rations which were generally unpalatable. The Irish pack rations were a God-send during the period of hostilities but the need to be supplemented by fresh rations – meats, vegetables, breads – was increasing in the aftermath of their cessation. This is where and when Captain Harry Crowley came into his own, his target now the upcoming Christmas dinner. Before that however, there were matters requiring attention and gendarmerie still had access to some portions of the city. It would be all too unfortunate should anything adverse happen now, especially after their precipitous induction to Katanga and the belligerence of the last ten days or so. All firing was suspended at 7.15am on the 19 December while the Katanga Government, the Congolese Central Government and the United Nations were engaged in peace talks. Meetings were held with Red Cross personnel in order to facilitate the distribution of food in the 36th Battalion area. The opportunity was availed of at this meeting to demonstrate that Irish troops did not loot private property but had sealed up to the best of their ability such houses as had been searched to assure Red Cross that Balubas were not allowed to loot or kill in any area controlled by the 36th Irish Battalion and to satisfy the Red Cross that white refugees who were old and infirm had been housed and fed.

The post office was still occupied in the morning by gendarmerie. They subsequently withdrew. The two Ethiopian battalions captured Union Miniere after first light; opposition was strong necessitating a full frontal assault resulting in heavy casualties. The control of refugees and the apprehension of suspects was continued. Civilians began moving freely in and out of the city. Unexploded mortar bombs were disposed of by ordnance officers in the different company localities over the following days during one of which the 8th and 35th Ethiopian Battalions were machine gunned and mortared for a considerable portion of a day. The International Red Cross began organising the distribution of foodstuffs to the civilian population and the Baluba refugees. White residents of the Irish battalion area who fled during the fighting were encouraged to visit their homes and remain. 'A' Company remained 'dug in', securing the tunnel. Lieutenant Sean Norton says of that time,

During the aftermath of the action at the tunnel, there were those, myself included, whose speech was slurred, and we kept talking quickly, very loud for days unceasingly. Another difficulty was an inability to sleep for some time afterwards. It was perhaps best described as a type of a high but one I would not want to experience again.

Meanwhile Captain Harry Crowley was hard at work doing the best deals for scarce petrol, getting the best cuts of meat at the battalion ration store, to the detriment of the other companies. There was also the barter method – flour for sliced pans, coffee and cocoa for mince meat, onions and milk for salami. It was a matter of getting the best from the rations. The unit history of the 36th Battalion records, 'Christmas Dinner was enjoyed by all'. They even had plum pudding thanks to some liberated dried fruit. 'C' Company replaced 'A' Company in the tunnel on the 28 December.

Notwithstanding, being relieved, 'A' Company were far from relaxed. Signalman Peter Fields remembers:

The month from the 16 December was quite intense and stressful, the tunnel and the railway line left and right of it had to be held; it was now precious to us, having lost two on the day of the taking of it. While the Christmas dinner was enormously enjoyable the 'Q' and cooks had worked wonders with the food, but up to early January the tempo was still up, only gradually and incrementally did it decrease. We did not know what was going to happen, if anything. We knew there was a truce, but what is a truce, only a temporary cessation of war. We were kept on our toes, there was a lot going on.

24

Keeping the Peace by Persuasion

THE VICTORY OF THE TUNNEL WASN'T GIVEN, IT WAS earned. Each soldier found something in him sufficient to close the matter out. 'A' Company had engaged in a remorseless exchange of fire, had been resilient, hadn't cracked, then during the thrust of things, found the tipping point with their repeated 84mm anti-tank fires and succeeded in sweeping speedily forward seizing on the half chance when presented. Maintaining the momentum by fighting through their objective, they went deep into the gendarmeries' rear, disrupting and harrying their hurried attempts to reorganise for a counter attack. They kept on harassing and fighting as reinforcements continued to arrive to concurrently engage individual groups of Irish occupied in clearance tasks as the impetus of the assault progressed.

What determined the outcome was determination itself — the contrasting differing degrees of it to be exact. Two factors assisted 'A' Company in their attack, namely that the tunnel defenders did not stand and fight to the last round and that, although they could have dug in extensively to very good effect, they did not do so. It would appear also that the mercenaries who manned the support weapons made their own individual private estimations of the situation and seeing the tide going against them took off with their support weapons for the communes (native villages outside the city) before Elisabethville became fully encircled.

Their overall plan of campaign, of harassment

tactics on the Irish and Swedish camps, the isolation of the Irish and Swedish from their lines of supply, and finally the seizure of the airport failed because the Irish and Swedish did not hole up in their camps but moved out towards them and by aggressive defence protected their camps successfully. Neither had they bargained on UN reinforcements coming in such strength to the Elisabethville area, (the two Ethiopian battalions, not needed to hold ground for defence, swung the balance of forces in the UN favour) and finally they had not reckoned that their own reinforcements from Kipushi and Jadotville would be denied to them by UN air and ground operations.

The UN troops now had the capability of employing 'fighting' or 'battle' patrols to dominate the city without 'occupying' it as such. The UN military would soon re-open the routes to the airport. The 'cease fire' was holding in the city, by and large; the time was ripe for the political situation to resume its dominance over the military scenario.

The main victory for the UN had been the capture, in great part, of world opinion as expressed in the world press. The various publics and people of influence now had a realisation of the Katangese irresponsibility and to accept the UN as the only stable element in the Congo. Efforts to effect the mobilisation of positive public opinion had been modest – little coordinated attempt to manage the strategic shaping of a positive perception existed as it was still early days for the UN in this regard – and although an immense and complex task, it was a vital one.

A Military Information Bureau at ONUC Headquarters did exist and the UN had in fact gone to great lengths in the avoidance of open conflict, yet heretofore the Katangese had been relatively successful portraying the UN as the aggressor. In order to continue to convince world opinion that the UN was still operating to prevent civil war and to assist the legal civil administration, all military operations had now to be subordinated to political factors. Public relations is, after all, the effect of behaviour on reputation. A clear picture, however, had not been successfully presented to the public. The Katangese were far more effective with their propaganda, busily bending the truth according to their needs. The UN was to learn that correcting misinformation effectively necessitates accurate, timely and complete information of your own. Also, it was not enough to counter the negative views, you had to also present the positive. Access to the media outlets hence to the many audiences internal and international was vital and not always as readily available as the UN hoped. Often when reached, the Katangese had their story in first and so the UN were reacting, and not proactive. Engagement did improve as time went on, the perception slowly caught up with the reality. It took events like the tunnel to make it so.

UN troops reverted to their original protective role: liaison with police for the restoration of public order and to protect the white population in the pursuit of their legal occupations. It had been found amongst the various types of prisoner captured that not all the UN's white opponents were mercenaries. Some whites fought because they believed they had no option but others had been convinced by their propaganda that the UN was evil and their troops were 'communists' – a ragbag term for all who opposed Katanga.

The situation remained troublesome in other areas as well as in Elizabethville where meanwhile the refugees were restive and great difficulty was experienced in controlling them. A war party of about two hundred Baluba Jeunesse from the refugee camp, armed with bows and arrows, knives and bicycle chains, attacked where they alleged two of their members had been murdered. The break-out was stopped at bayonet point by a platoon of 'C' Company under Captain Keyes. The UN having at last gained a hard-earned favourable reputation, the 36th Battalion reverting to keeping the peace had now still to do so by persuasion. They had to now take off the 'steel gloves' and put back on the 'soft' ones. The refugee camp had originated as a direct result of hostile measures taken by the Katangese authorities against people whom they considered to be aliens. These people were, in the main, Balubas from the province of Kasai. They were reputed to be the most intelligent of the Congolese people and indeed they held some very good positions in Elisabethville, as teachers, clerical workers and the like. Their first reaction to the threats of violence to themselves and their families was of course to seek refuge with the UN. Those first threatened appeared to be the most well-to-do. They flocked to the Swedish and Irish camps. The Swedes, who had more accommodation in their camp, gave refuge, however, the numbers became so great that the 36th Battalions' predecessors, the 35th Battalion, were asked to establish a camp in the vicinity of the Irish lines. This was done and with the camp established shortly after it's commencement an outbreak occurred in a Katangese prison just south of Elisabethville. Approximately six hundred and fifty prisoners escaped, all of whom made their way to UN camps, including those injured in the outbreak. They claimed protection and asserted that they had been held as political prisoners. Undoubtedly some were political, but many were just ordinary criminals. The Katangese authorities asked that these prisoners be handed back to them; this request was refused by the UN. The ex-prisoners were housed at a location known as the 'Factory' which had been vacated by 'C' Company in an effort to concentrate the Battalion in the vicinity of Leopold Farm. A platoon of 'C' Company remained in the 'Factory' as a guard over the ex-prisoners. After approximately three weeks in this camp the ex-prisoners were transferred to a section of their own adjacent to the main refugee camp. During their stay in the 'Factory' the refugees were very well behaved and co-operated in every way possible. It soon became apparent that the refugees were too numerous, and would have to be moved to another location and the residential area which they had inundated, cleared.

The Swedish and Irish Battalions undertook the task of moving thousands of people to the newly selected location where the refugees set about constructing their own shelters. With the commencement of the refugee problem the medical staff of the battalion was constantly engaged in attending to the stream of refugees who reported daily for medical attention. The Chaplain was busily engaged also giving spiritual and material assistance by performing normal rites of the Church and in uniting families and in bringing about better conditions for the refugees. In this latter task he was assisted from time-to-time by numerous officers, NCOs and men of the battalion. As time progressed many of the refugees who had relatives or work in other parts of the Congo were sent there by plane. A camp commandant was appointed (Swedish) and the defence of the camp apportioned equally between the Irish and Swedish battalions. In time civilian experts in refugee work became associated with the camp. There were among the refugees the youths known as the 'Jeunesse' who were a constant source of trouble. They made frequent attacks on Katangese police and at one stage became bold enough to attack Swedish patrols and threaten Irish sentries. Joint patrols of Swedish, Irish and Katangese police were initiated and continued up to the December fighting at which point they abruptly ceased. The rainy season and the renewal of hostilities brought much hardship to the refugees; many were killed by deliberate sniping and mortaring of the camp. Attempts were made to locate the snipers and mortar positions, but they were constantly on the move. Whenever it was possible food and clothing were given to the refugees. The strength of the refugee camp was estimated at 35,000 to 40,000.

Keeping the camps habitable and sanitary, handling of stores and looking to the tactical requirements, guards, patrols and escorts were all sources of continuous heavy work, as was the maintenance of camp defences; the mix of sunshine, tropical rain and electric storms all taking their toll. Billeted now in the unlikely setting of an abandoned maternity hospital, the pace of peacekeeping was preferable to the hostility and trauma of the fighting. Replacing the racket of the mortar and machine-gun fire was the quietness and stillness of the African night. This ironically presented a strangeness of its own. Through the tranquillity became apparent the barks and growls of prowling wild dogs and other animals not yet settled down for the night. Suddenly the sentries became aware of a stranger sound still, superseding the proceedings, a clear Irish tenor voice in what, for the circumstances, was a remarkable performance of *My Mary of the Curling Hair*; Corkman Corporal Dan Mannix was giving an impromptu rendition of his favourite song. Men gathered and joined in, harmonising, and gradually a collective voice was heard. It was exactly what was needed and developed to the stage of a sing-song every night accompanying the ration of sweets, cigarettes and beer.

Elsewhere, the gendarmerie started the murder of Balubas in the communes, and Guerrilla warfare was also organised among tribes in Katanga against ONUC. Gendarmerie would sometimes become active in the city (Elisabethville) and try to take up or take over positions in the city. They also tried to capture ONUC personnel. Plans were finalised for the departure of the Katanga Government to Kipushi while the advance party of the Tunisian battalion arrived at Elisabethville airport. Refugees continued to loot property, Irish patrols intervening once discovered.

The arrival of the New Year saw the gendarmerie south of the city while the UN operational area was divided into zones in which each battalion was responsible for patrolling to ensure dominance of its area and security of life and property. The Irish responsibility was extensive; not alone did the 36th Battalion patrol within its own area, but also had responsibility in the Ethiopian and Indian zones. Affairs in the Congo not yet settled, it was however back to 'keeping the peace', albeit by persuasion.

25

Stand Tall

THOSE WHO WENT OUT AS BOYS CAME BACK MEN, those who went out men came back better men, was how Private, now Quartermaster Sergeant (retd) Jim 'Nobby' Clarke (a driver with 'A' Company) summed it all up. His family history is heavily populated with military connections, his father whose six brothers and a sister all served in the British Army during either World War I and World War II, all survived. His maternal grandfather and his brother William Armstrong served with the Royal Dublin Fusiliers during the Boer War, the latter was killed and his name is inscribed on the Fusiliers Arch entrance to Saint Stephen's Green, Dublin. CQMS Clarke had three sons who served in the Irish Army. Those surviving 'men' and 'boys' of the battle of the tunnel Elisabethville Congo 16 December 1961 are today grandparents and great-grandparents, as is Major-General (retd) Vincent Savino President of IUNVA (Irish United Nations Veterans Association) who himself saw service in the Congo May to November 1962 as a staff officer in ONUC HQ Leopoldville.

Before Congo, life in the Defence Forces was best described as drudgery, a day-to-day routine of boredom, duties and inspections. I filled my time with a heavy involvement in sports and, fortunately, being a training officer in the Cadet School I had a felt purpose.

When Congo came there was, throughout the Defence

Forces, a sudden surge of excitement, a great uplifting of optimism, and an intense curiosity. This feeling pervaded into Irish public life as well, witnessed by the huge crowds that turned out to see the departing battalions parading through Dublin's city centre en route to Baldonnel for their airlift to Africa. Our, and indeed the entire country's confidence got a major, immediate boost. Straight away we were making history and earned a high regard in Ireland and over a short time abroad. While we had to learn many new things operating in a very different role, unfamiliar theatre, and at a much higher tempo, there was a definite and sudden realism that our core training stood to us; we were as good as anybody else (if not better) and this percolated into the country. Our ability to communicate and connect, particularly with the local people was innate and very important. Standards started to lift as soldiers of theory became soldiers of practice and self-belief. Suddenly on the training grounds, the section rooms, the barrack squares, the exercise areas, the amateurness of our approach was gone. Suddenly we were applying the training, the drills, the skills, the equipment with an associated real purpose and real meaning. This was matched by a real fear of 'what next after Congo?' Only for a great exhalation of relief, 'we're going again'; Cyprus opened up.

Mistakes were made, lessons learned, equipment purchased, combat experienced; the Irish emerged up-skilled and far wiser, infinitely more discerning about competing interests, political and commercial, and the many powerful agendas at play, the obvious and less so. Lessons learned in the field are not easily forgotten. No amount of training could equal the actual exercising of military skills in the field. The Irish came back from the

Congo as better soldiers and better people, better aware of the interdependency at the unit's core, vital to the make up of all working units, and much better aware of one's own place in the bigger picture. Nowhere was this more obvious than in the newly recognised importance of the doctor, the chaplain, the engineer, the welfare officer, the cook, the tailor, the driver, the fitter, the signaller, the leaders. They came home too with a new appreciation of the importance of fresh water, fruit, vegetables and meat. Horizons had been expanded, real life problems of a unit in the field had been experienced, in a totally strange and hostile environment. How to interpret and implement the mission, the exercising of the logistic function, the medical care of personnel in a hostile place, managing movement, maintenance of transport and communications, the management of the operation in all its aspects.

The Defence Forces and – it's not too strong a suggestion to make – the Irish nation had come of age. Participation in the Congo operation was for the Irish their first major involvement in international community affairs, advancing earlier diplomatic efforts and developments with the United Nations, and required a change in domestic legislation to allow Defence Forces units to serve abroad. This new role granted the Irish an international involvement and was an unprecedented undertaking. It was exciting and connected the people by its scale to spectacular events abroad in the name of Ireland, first fostering, and then enhancing a positive sense of self amongst the nation. Subsequent news of the nine deaths resulting from the Niemba Ambush in November 1960, four months after their celebratory exhilaration of departure brought shock and an outpouring of genuine grief across the country, yet the sorrow was a *mood as much merged with pride as it was sadness. The tragedy was not to discourage further participation nor deter future participants, the Irish continuing to live up to the commitment of their believed obligations to the United Nations ideal of promoting the cause of international peace, specifically maintaining order in far away Congo. The next most comparable distinguishing event as dramatic, more pragmatic than ideal, was the country's 1973 entry to the EEC. Yet there was a concrete pragmatism also in the men of the pro- and anti-treaty traditions finding common ground continuing that of 'the call to arms' during the emergency years 1939-1946, and saluting their Irish soldiers taking part in a peacekeeping force with the UN. This overseas peacekeeping service was a whole new dimension for the Defence Forces, a completely new outward-looking dynamic which dramatically increased their experience, enhanced their morale, extended their horizons far beyond anything heretofore imagined and in so doing immeasurably improved the country's international standing.*

For many of the young men of 'A' Company, who fought, faced fire, whose friends became fatalities, their future was to see them standing tall, again wearing the blue beret, in other mission areas around the world, for that is what they do, who they are, what they became. Others chose different walks of life but unfailingly every year on the Sunday nearest to the 16 December they meet and remember the tunnel. Now 50 years on, sadly with each passing year their number is fewer, the occasion becoming ever more noteworthy, a moving landmark remembrance of camaraderie. On return to Ireland in the early summer of 1962 'A' Company members didn't talk to many people about the early eventful days of their tour of duty. The tunnel attack had its share of media exposure at the time of its occurrence and for a while afterwards. Now 50 years later, rationalising these phenomena Signalman Peter Fields suggested it was because 'It belonged to us', its achievement was because of our togetherness and the professionalism of those who led. They were what I call black and white men; they knew what had to be done in the circumstances and they knew how to do it. The NCOs were genuine, not to be crossed, a bit gruff but good. We were young and impressionable; they and the old soldiers were father figures and really looked after us. This togetherness was why we succeeded. This is why still today that camaraderie has lasted.

26

Power and Peace

WHILE THE IRISH ARMY AND PEOPLE COULD STAND
tall with a justifiable pride in their new found
peacekeeping skills, they could only do so momentarily
in an as yet very unsettled arena. The capture of the
tunnel successfully decided the second Battle of
Katanga and in truth proved the vital turning point
in favour of the UN's overall Congolese peacekeeping
campaign. There was, one year later, a third albeit
somewhat lesser Battle of Katanga, the UN having
to forcefully affirm its authority and the Irish again
featured prominently. The 38th Battalion under
Lieutenant Colonel Paddy Delaney (later Chief of
Staff) found itself back in the firing line at Kibushi.
Specifically Captain (later Colonel) Tom O'Boyle
and his Heavy Mortar Troop (Hy Mor Tp) of 120mm
mortars were under command of the Indian Brigade.
On the 29 December 1962, the 3rd Ethiopian Brigade
captured Simba Hill en route to Kipushi. Five days
previously on Christmas Eve, a UN helicopter had
been shot down over Karavia, one Indian officer
killed and five badly beaten. Also, firing commenced
from gendarmerie on UN positions, mainly south of
the capital. Now, five days later the 38th Battalion,
conducting a passage of lines, passed through the
Ethiopians on Simba Hill, the way paved by fires
on both sides of their axis of advance from Captain
O'Boyle's mortar troop in support. On arrival at
Kafuba Bridge they found it had just been blown-

up. The Indian Field Engineer Company built a new bridge, and so enabled the Irish Battalion to enter the town unopposed the following morning, the mercenaries and gendarmerie having fled hurriedly overnight leaving large stocks of food, equipment, weapons, ammunition, important documents and fuel behind. The UN forces' subsequent actions were to pursue and push the aggressors across the Rhodesian border. The Irish Heavy Mortar Troop was continuously in action in the various engagements from 28 December 1962 to 21 January 1963.

In May 1964 the Irish involvement in ONUC ceased and on the 30 June 1964 the United Nations force in the Congo withdrew according to plan, completing the military phase of ONUC. The secession of Katanga had successfully been prevented. The integrity of the inclusivity of an all tribal and provincial Congo was preserved, from which emerged a western-friendly Mobutu regime in Leopoldville. Mosie Tshombe who had fled across the Rhodesian border during Operation Morthor returned to be given a Ministerial role.

Within a year of the UN's departure however, the inclusivity deal disintegrated; Joseph Mobutu, privately assured of US support, seized the moment, abolished parliament, and with the Force Publique under his personal control took a firm hold of power. Adopting an anti-communist stance his pro-western pro-business policies saw the mining interests resuming business un-interfered with for annual payments. Africa was Africa; it was all about power, not peace. Decades of rebellions and coups followed.

The Irish Defence Forces' experience in the Congo had been likened to a classroom where lessons were learned, and while they certainly were, it is however more true to say it was nearer to an examination where they were torridly tested, under severe scrutiny, to be passed or failed, with soldiers living or dying. Twenty-six did die, 19 killed in action. Like any appraisal it granted an opportunity to prove themselves in a combat situation. Coming under fire is an initiation, unlike that in any other walk of life. The Irish acquitted themselves well, with honour and gained a hard-earned respect, in particular demonstrating fairness, decency and empathy with the indigenous peoples. The UN identified the Irish as highly suitable peacekeepers, to be further deployed in the future throughout the world's trouble spots.

The UN intervention into the Congolese Civil War probably prevented the super-powers coming into confrontation over the Congo. Order however had sometimes to be restored by force and was costly in lives lost, 126 UN peacekeepers, its Secretary General Dag Hammarskjöld and many hundreds, perhaps thousands of Congolese. Costly too in terms of expense, over four hundred million dollars. Lost also was perhaps optimism about what peacekeeping per se of itself could achieve as a number of key elements to the success of peacekeeping were absent. If the cooperation of parties is missing and they or one of the parties remains determined to continue to fight, there is no peace to be kept. If the UN force is mandated, justified and willing to use force it then has to have a tolerance for casualties and fundamentally must be an effective force to begin with.

The parties' cooperation, the UN forces competency, its impartiality, an appropriate and meaningful mandate, little or no outside interference or other external factors are all elements, amongst others, necessary to be in place to give effect to what peacekeeping can offer, their absence making an already difficult job far more complex, and is all too frequently the case. Decidedly, however, a lasting peace must be the goal to be attained by the in-country conflicting parties, whereas power is all too often their goal. A country's resources, but resource of leadership particularly, are elements for consideration too; the former not necessary, the latter crucial. Political power controls the resources, an enlightened leadership will grant access to this economic power, an unenlightened one holds and maintains this monopoly and so sows the seeds for those completely excluded to continue to pursue by force their interests in the absence of any alternative, and the cycle continues. There were many challenges then to the implementation of peacekeeping in the Congo and subsequently no shortage of critics who claimed the UN intervention as a failure, whether or which, it was not the peacekeepers who were found wanting. The men of 'A' Company who crossed their start line advancing towards the tunnel on that forlorn wet, dark winter's morning on 16 December 1961 endured the dangers and by force of arms, fought for the power that peace grants, hope, and they won. It, the power of peace, was a noble victory.

Epilogue

BLIGHTED BY INSECURITY SINCE GAINING independence in 1960, the Democratic Republic of Congo (DRC), although vast and hugely rich in agriculture and mineral resources remained disunited, underdeveloped, and was undemocratically governed, so had continually failed to function as a state proper. Centralised power remained persistent over the people's popular consent. This continuity of non-unified, non-functionality preferred over stability predominated; as a result, an incohesive Congo today remains a country which has yet to experience democratic local elections. Meanwhile conditions for conflict persisted in Congo's volatile eastern provinces, land and mineral resources central to the combatant's cause. Un-reconciled to democracy, the pursuit of power (and profit) came before the people. The situation in the Congo was and remains linked to that of the region as a whole. The Democratic Republic of Congo was, and is, in a fragile state as a consequence of internal turmoil and outside interference. External influences in the form of the Rwandan government's interests are a consideration; also relations with Angola are tense, a dispute involving offshore oil and maritime borders persists, while potential for conflict with Uganda on a number of issues continues. Today almost all of Katanga's mineral resources go to China, and Chinese involvement with the whole of the Democratic Republic of the Congo looks set to increase; currently half of all the country's exports go to China. Korean infrastructure companies also are becoming increasingly involved with the DRC.

A UN mission MONUSCO, Mission de l'organisation des nations Unies pour la stabilisation en République Démocratique du Congo, is in place. They are assisting in the disarming, demobilising and re-integrating the DRC's half dozen or so various rival militias into an army concerning itself with internal issues of security arising from those militias as yet un-reconciled. These UN peacekeepers must be sensitive to the political context but more so to those parties prepared to risk confrontation when it suits. Such continued conflict has adversely impacted on international interest to invest there, shrinking the country's economy while the population has grown to in excess of fifty million. Still vastly wealthy and rich today as ever in minerals, uranium, copper, cobalt, gold, diamonds, oil and other resources. These and enormous rainforests, fertile land and harnessable rivers for hydroelectric power supply, the country's potential for economic growth remains massive but unfulfilled. However, the series of peace agreements signed in 2002 resulted in elections in 2006 only to see violence erupt in 2007 between the personal militia of the losing candidate (Jean-Pierre Bamba) and government forces of President Joseph Kabilas' regime. Such tensions are expected to be evident again in the run up to presidential elections (scheduled for November 2011); the country's political transition still a work in progress.

On Katanga's high plateau in south western Congo is the watershed for the two largest rivers in Africa,

the Congo and the Zambezi. Half a century ago
involvement in Katanga and the Congo was to be a
watershed for the UN, accentuating the stark reality of
the acute difference between peacekeeping and peace-
enforcement; and for Ireland, in the choosing of the
dividing line between isolation from, to involvement
in, world affairs. The UN's and Ireland's involvement in
what was a major world event became a defining chapter
in the annals of their respective early formations. The
Congo marked a significant turning point for the UN
in its maintaining of so large and daring a peacekeeping
force, and for Ireland its first ever troop involvement in
a military operation into a mission area. Both for the
UN and Ireland that peacekeeping participation and
involvement in the Congo represented a steep learning
curve in the organisation's and state's brief history
and was to prove to be a bruising experience. A loss
of innocence was suffered by the initial breath-taking
mismatching of on-ground military realities with ever-
changing political priorities; and the going on the
offensive without the proper military capability and
assets to project force; but to progress you have always
got to be in motion, the application had to catch up
with the aspiration and neither did the UN nor Ireland
shrink from the immensity of the task put in front of
them.

Between 20 July 1960 and 15 May 1964 more than
six thousand Irish soldiers served in the Congo and for
the first time since the Civil War, and before that the
War of Independence, Irish soldiers became involved
in heavy fighting. Fatalities and serious casualties
were suffered, yet many demonstrated bravery, others

outright heroism, all faced the challenges and sacrifices of service thousands of miles from home, emerging much experienced and vastly more discerning. With the involvement followed wisdom from the realisation that the Defence Forces, in exposing its soldiers to the threat of potential and actual combat, would henceforth have a fulsome operational appreciation of the value of modern armaments, air support and armoured assets, logistical and operational co-ordination and training and leadership skills. But there also resulted an unspoken pride and self-respect as a hard-won little-mentioned self-belief followed. A quiet knowledge emerged that they had faced a sudden, shocking, severe test, and passed. Irish soldiers had acquitted themselves when it mattered. Moreover, had shown an empathy and understanding of the suffering of the ordinary indigenous people, a quality that was to become their hallmark. The Congo involvement thereby laid the basis for a reputation that has endured and that over seventy three missions world-wide and 50 years later has been enhanced.

The Congo continues as a troubled and chaotic country. Both despite, and perhaps because of, it's vast mineral wealth, with fighting, rebellions and atrocities being part of its brutal history. It remains a noteworthy hotspot with much blame, bitterness and bewilderment arising.

The UN's first operation in the Congo, if not an outright lasting triumph was nonetheless a victory. It ceased the attempted secession of Moise Tshombes' Katanga Province with his mercenary-led army and so prevented the outright fragmentation of the Congo, facilitating the fledgling state's right to a continued existence as a complete entity. It granted the Congolese time and space, opportunity and hope to aspire towards a meaningful self-determination. Significantly the UN, in aspiring its ideals, demonstrated it's willingness to back them.

Glossary

ANC	Armée Nationale Congolaise (the army of the newly independent Democratic Republic of Congo)
APC	Armoured Personnel Carrier
APOD	Airport of Disembarkation
Baluba	Congolese Tribe
CB	Counter Battery (Mortar Fires)
EEC	European Economic Community (1973) Ireland's entry date
Etat Major	Gendarmerie/Mercenary Headquarters in Elisabethville
FN	Fabrique National (Belgian Arms Manufacturer)

FOO	Forward Observation Officer
GPMG	General Purpose Machine Gun
HMG	Heavy Machine gun
HQ	Headquarters
IUNVA	Irish United Nations Veterans Association
JAMBO	Katangese Gendarmerie
MFC	Mobile Fire Controller
NCO	Non Commissioned Officer (Corporals, Sergeants mostly)
OC	Officer Commanding
ONUC	Opérations des Nations Unies au Congo (United Nations Operation in the Congo)
SL	Start Line
SLR	Self Loading Rifle
Re-org	Reorganisation location having secured the objective
UN	United Nations
UNIFIL	United Nations Interim Force in Lebanon

PRESENT DAY PLACE NAMES	
1961	**2011**
The Congo	Democratic Republic of Congo (DRC)
Elizabethville	Lubumbashi
Leopoldville	Kinshasa
Albertville	Kalemie
Jadotville	Likasi
Stanleyville	Kisangani
Lubuaboury	Kananga
Rhodesia	Zimbabwe
Katanga	Katanga
Kolwezi	Kolwezi

Chronology of Significant Events

DATE	EVENT
1884	Berlin Conference organised by German Chancellor Otto Von Bismarck in November to prevent potential disputes between colonial powers over as yet unclaimed regions of Africa. King Leopold II of Belgium is personally granted enormous tracts of Congolese territory.
1885	Congo Free State formally established under King Leopold II (of Belgium).
1900	King Leopold II monopolisation of Congolese trade in rubber especially, to supply demand for tyres arising from development of automobiles.
1903	Allegations of appalling abuse and atrocities of native Congolese, subject to punishments for failing to meet laid down quotas by overseers is made public in May by American missionary William Morrison causing public outrage, especially in Britain. Roger Casement British Consul in the Congo is directed to undertake investigation. His report released in December reveals shocking detailed confirmation of abuses committed, causing widespread condemnation and criticism. Roger Casement is subsequently knighted for his work.
1908	Congo Free State annexed by Belgium.
1913	Copper deposits discovered in Katanga. Other major mineral deposits, including diamonds also unearthed.

DATE	EVENT
1914	Outbreak of WWI, German occupation of Belgium.
1940	Further occupation of Belgium by the German's during WWII weakens their circumstances until war ends in 1945.
1959	Belgium's King Bedouin visits Congo after a decade of unrest, strikes, disturbances, even a mutiny by Force Publique, and a prior announcement (1952) by Governor General Léon Antoine Marie P'etillon that civil rights reform is required. This visit is not a success as he is blamed for delaying independence.
1960	Congo gains independence in June. The following month Moise Tshombe leads Katanga secession attempt. Congo's new Prime Minister Patrice Lumumba appeals to the Un for support. The UN agrees to send troops. Ireland contributes two peacekeeping contingents. Deposed in a coup in September Patrice Lumumba is later killed (January 1961). Two months later (November) 9 Irish soldiers killed by Baluba tribesmen at an ambush at Niemba, Northern Katanga.
1961	Following the murder of Patrice Lumumba in January, a new UN resolution is passed in February allowing for use of force. In August UN operation Rampunch's initial successes are not capitalised upon. The following month Operation Morthor results in conflict. UN Secretary General Dag Hammarskjöld dies in aircraft crash en route to negotiations. 'A' Company 35 Bn put up a determined four-day resistance in Jadotville. In December UN Operation UNOKAT in which the Irish Operation Sarsfield successfully sees an Irish offensive action secure the Tunnel in Elisabethville. Tshombe flees.

DATE	EVENT
1962	UN Operation Grand Slam (September – December) sees off finally any further military attempts in support of Katangese secession, an Irish involvement at Kibushi is successful. Tshombe flees again.
1963	Political rivalry emerges between President Joseph Kasavubu and General Joseph Mobutu commander of the Force Publique. Congolese parliament is suspended.
1964	Congolese central government becomes inclusive and allows Tshombe to take up a post within it. The UN mission is wound up and Irish troop commitment to ONUC ends in June.
1965	Tshombe sacked from Government in May and one month later Joseph Mobutu stages a coup. He remains pre-western and pro-business for the next twenty-two years, having in 1977 renamed his country 'Zaire'. (River that swallows all rivers).
1994	Rwanda erupts, Hutus attack Tutsis, one million are savagely butchered in massacres.
1996	Tutsis regrouped, attack Hutus who flee Rwanda, Tutsis control large portions of eastern Zaire. An ill Mobutu cannot control the situation and Uganda begins to take mineral resources from eastern Zaire by backing rebel leader Laurent-Désiré Kabila.
1997	Mobutu flees Zaire and dies in exile in Morocco. Kabila resumes power.
1998	Troops from Angola, Namibia and Zimbabwe support Kabila's forces against a Rwandan-led rebel offensive. Further support from Chad, Sudan and Libya continues to prop up Kabila.

DATE	EVENT
2001	A protracted stalemate continued until assignation of Kabila, nonetheless hostilities continue. New President Joseph Kabila takes over. UN force MONUC arrives in March.
2002	Withdrawal of outside troops commences.
2003	Interim Multinational Emergency Forces of 1,500 EU troops ('Operation Artémis') assists MONUC.
2005	President Joseph Kabila discusses investment with China and South Korea on visits there.
2006	Integration of six militia groups into new unified national army commences. In late July another 1,500 EU force is deployed, to ensure election safety. President Joseph Kabila is successfully elected, promising social, economic and political reforms.
2008	Renegade General Laurent Nkunda clashes with DRC forces.
2009	Congolese and Rwandan militaries launch joint operation against renegade forces.
2010	MONUC becomes MONUSCO and prepares to begin drawdown of forces.
2011	Presidential elections scheduled for November 2011.

An Bonn Seirbhíse Dearscna
The Distinguished Service Medal

On 18 February 1964 a medal to be known as 'An Bonn Seirbhíshe Dearscna' or, in English, 'The Distinguished Service Medal', was introduced by the Defence Forces. The medal may be awarded to officers, non-commissioned officers and privates of the Defence Forces and to members of the Army Nursing and Chaplaincy Services in recognition of individual or associated acts of bravery, courage, leadership, resource or devotion to duty (other than any such acts or duty performed on war service) arising out of, or associated with, service in the Defence Forces and not meriting the award of An Bonn Míleata Calmachta.

The medal may be awarded in the following classes:
with **Honour;**
with **Distinction;**
with **Merit**.

The medal in any one of the classes prescribed shall not be awarded more than once to any one person but, for each succeeding act sufficient to justify a further award in the same class, a **bar to the medal** in that class may be awarded.

The Distinguished Service Medal Citations

WITH HONOUR

81244 Corporal Charles Connolly

'For distinguished service with the UNITED Nations Force in the Republic of Congo, by acts of bravery and devotion to duty under fire as a medical orderly, during December, 1961, in the Elizabethville area. Regardless of his own safety, he attended casualties under heavy mortar and small arms fire during which a non-commissioned Officer was seriously wounded and later died. On another occasion, on his own initiative, he crossed open country swept by fire to render first aid. In this action an Officer and Soldier died, but despite the danger involved, Corporal Connelly continued to bring medical aid to others who were wounded.'

WITH DISTINCTION

O.6378 Commandant Joseph Fitzpatrick

'For distinguished service with the United Nations Force in the Republic of Congo, in displaying courage and leadership when securing an important position in Elizabethville on 16 December 1961. The leading platoon suffered casualties, but Commandant Fitzpatrick exposed himself repeatedly to fire and, by his personal

courage, energy and leadership, maintained the impetus of
the advance until the objective was attained.'

O.7776 Lieutenant Patrick Riordan

'For distinguished service with the United Nations
Force in the Republic of Congo, in displaying courage and
leadership during the period of hostilities in December
1961. Lieutenant Riordan was tireless in his task in
insuring the efficiency and welfare of his platoon under very
trying circumstances, and it was while actually leading his
platoon in an attack that he met his death.'

O.7806 Lieutenant Sean Norton

'For distinguished service with the United Nations Force
in the Republic of Congo, for leadership and courage. From
08 to 16 December 1961, immediately on its arrival in
Elizabethville, Lieutenant Norton's platoon was involved
in active operations. The platoon displayed efficiency,
aggressiveness and high morale under heavy fire, and this
was due to Captain Norton's leadership and courage. His
disregard for his personal safety and his tireless energy were
an inspiration to his men.'

O.7887 Lieutenant Peter Feely

'For distinguished service with the United Nations
Force in the Republic of Congo, in displaying courage and

leadership. From the time of his arrival in the Congo, Lieutenant Feely was engaged in action and he displayed coolness and control at all times. When his platoon was ordered to clear snipers from railway carriages in Elizabethville, he personally handled the task, dashing in close to the carriages, lobbing grenades through the windows before entering the carriages to clear them.'

810957 Corporal Gerald Francis

'For distinguished service with the United Nations Force in the Republic of Congo, in displaying leadership and courage under fire. During the period of hostilities in December 1961, when his platoon commander had been killed and he himself had been wounded, Corporal Francis remained with his section and successfully completed his tasks.'

808720 Corporal Patrick Gregan

'For distinguished service with the United Nations Force in the Republic of Congo, for courage and devotion to duty. On 16 December 1961, he deliberately exposed himself to heavy automatic fire on a number of occasions in order to use his own 84 mm anti-tank rifle more effectively. His courageous action and accurate fire were of great assistance to his platoon and helped it to complete it's mission without heavy casualties. Later in the action, *although wounded, he continued until ordered back for treatment.'*

WITH MERIT

87410 Sergeant Patrick Mulcahy

'For distinguished service with the United Nations Force in the Republic of the Congo, in displaying leadership and devotion to duty to a high degree. Although painfully wounded during hostilities in December 1961, he refused to leave his platoon and subsequently whilst looking after his men, he received the wound from which he died.'

808427 Corporal James Fallon

'For distinguished service with the United Nations Force in the Republic of the Congo, in displaying devotion to duty to a high degree. The then Private Fallon insisted in remaining with his platoon although his brother had been killed in action. He displayed character, leadership and initiative to such an extent that he was promoted during his period of service overseas.'

809418 Sergeant Daniel Mannix

'For distinguished service with the United Nations Force in the Republic of the Congo, in displaying devotion to duty on several periods of service. Sergeant Mannix, then a Corporal, distinguished himself by the care and time which he devoted to his men. During active operations, his leadership and control were of a high order.'

809456 Sergeant John Ryan

'For distinguished service with the United Nations Force in the Republic of the Congo, in displaying devotion to duty while serving as a wireless operator during a period of hostilities. Sergeant Ryan, then a Corporal, succeeded in maintaining communications despite difficult and hazardous conditions and by his skill, composure and devotion to duty, played a major part in the success of his battalion's operations.'

78854 Private Peter Madigan

'For distinguished service with the United Nations Force in the Republic of the Congo, for outstanding devotion to duty over several periods of service. Private Madigan's loyalty, steadiness and general trustworthiness made him a very valuable man wherever he served, and these attributes, together with his devotion to duty, proved to be a steadying and beneficial influence on his fellow soldiers.'

806014 Private James Murray

'For distinguished service with the United Nations Force in the Republic of the Congo, in displaying devotion to duty and courage. During a period of hostilities in December 1961, Private Murray, a cook, repeatedly endangered himself in bringing food to the troops under fire. On one occasion, a container of food was blown out of his hands by a mortar bomb, yet he returned immediately with a fresh supply.'

806540 Corporal Anthony Woodcock

'For distinguished service with the United Nations Force in the Republic of the Congo, in displaying leadership and devotion to duty during the period December 1961 to May 1962, Corporal Woodcock, then a private soldier was an example to his comrade soldiers by his calmness and initiative. Although painfully wounded at one stage, he insisted that another wounded soldier receive treatment before himself and displayed calmness and fortitude which had a considerable effect on the remainder of the platoon.'

Roll of Honour

Cpl M Fallon *Killed in Action on 8 Dec 1961.*
Lt P Riordan DSM *Killed in Action 16 Dec 1961.*
Pte A Wickham *Killed in Action on 16 Dec 1961.*
Sgt P Mulcahy DSM *Died on 16 Dec 1961 from wounds received in action.*
Cpl J Power *Died in the Congo on 7 Mar 1962 from natural causes.*

The following members of 'A' Company 36th Infantry Battalion were injured:
Capt H Agnew
Cpl G Francis
Cpl S Gregan
Cpl T Gorman
Cpl A Woodcock
Pte A Confrey
Pte J Desmond
Pte J Dunne
Tpr O Fergus
Pte P Gilrain
Pte G Kelly
Tpr M McMullan
Pte W Marsh
Pte M Raftery